Demerara Sugar

Demerara Sugar

Pam Walters

Rock's Mills Press
Oakville, Ontario
2020

A BRIEF NOTE ON NAMES AND PLACES

Throughout this book I refer to "Guiana," a commonly used abbreviated form of "British Guiana," the British colony in South America formed in 1831 by the union of three smaller colonies—Demerara, Essequibo, and Berbice. In 1966, British Guiana gained its independence from the UK, becoming the new nation of Guyana. Guyana is part of a larger region on the northeastern coast of South America often referred to as the Guianas, which includes Guyana itself; French Guiana, an overseas department of France; Suriname, now an independent republic but formerly a Dutch possession, when it was known as Surinam or Dutch Guiana; the Guyana Region in Venezuela; and the Brazilian state of Amapá, which was known as Portuguese Guiana in colonial times.

Published by
Rock's Mills Press
www.rocksmillspress.com

For information, please contact us at customer.service@rocksmillspress.com or visit us online at www.rocksmillspress.com.

To Stephen and Mark

With thanks for the memories …

The happy, happy memories!

Foreword

Sugar was not always the evil substance that it is today. Only relatively recently has it been acknowledged to rot the teeth, pile on the pounds and shorten life. It is interesting to note that in the First Century A.D., Pliny the Elder declared that 'sugar is used for medicinal purposes only.' One wonders what the health of the world's population would be like had man paid heed to those words.

Once, sugar was a rarity. It was a commodity available only to kings, emperors and the mega-rich. The sugar-cane was famously described as 'the reed that gives honey without bees'—honey being, of course, the original sweetener and available only to those who knew how to procure it. At that time it was only the juice pressed from the sugar-cane plant that was used as a sweetener. As a sweet treat the cane could be cut into small portions and the juice sucked from it (it still is). These small portions, sucked dry of their juice and baked even drier in the sun, were used by the poor to clean their teeth—a forerunner of the toothbrush.

Sugar exists in green plants, fruits and vegetables but in sugar-cane and beet it is found in abundance which is why only cane sugar and beet sugar are produced in commercial quantities. It is said to have been originally 'discovered' in Polynesia by the Persian Emperor, Darius (it was he who referred to 'honey without bees') when the Persians invaded India in 510 B.C., although it is thought to have existed in that country for centuries before that date. 'Since time immemorial' are the words often used. Darius and the Persians were careful never to broadcast their discovery. It was kept secret, a very closely guarded secret, which enabled those in the know to become fabulously rich. However, in 642 B.C., also as a result of invasion, the Arabs found sugar-cane plants growing and sugar being produced in India. The Arabs were more generous with their findings, taking their knowledge to the countries they conquered and planting sugar-cane there. These included warmer places like North Africa and Spain, although neither was ideal for growing the plant and it was hundreds of years before the perfect climate was found.

It was not until the 11th Century that Europeans generally became aware of the existence of sugar. The Crusaders returned from the wars with amazing tales of places they had been, sights they had seen, food they had eaten—and they were particularly keen on something they called a 'spice' or a 'sweet spice' (they could think of no other name for it) which could be used to enhance the taste of food. Some Crusaders even took this 'sweet spice' back home. This first record of sugar in England dates from 1099.

Sugar remained a luxury as the sugar-cane plant did not thrive in the European climate and the commodity could not be produced in large quantities. It was found that the liquid, when boiled down, left a residue of solids, known to the Indians as 'Sakhara' which is the Sanscrit word for 'gravel'. The larger solids were called 'Khand' from which we now have the word 'Candy.'

Columbus, on his first voyage of exploration in 1492, stopped at the island of La Gomera in the Canary Islands, where his ships picked up supplies for their forward journey. They were meant to stay there for four days but remained for a month. Columbus' second voyage to the New World took place in 1493, which seems a remarkably swift turnaround for sailing ships in the 15th Century. The reason for this seems to have been largely by-passed by historians who recorded the explorer's voyages. It was said that Columbus and the lady Governor of La Gomera had become romantically involved.

The Governor was Beatriz de Bobadilla y Ossorio, the widow of the previous Governor, who was acting as regent for her young son until he became old enough to take his father's place. Images of her show Beatriz to be an extraordinarily beautiful young woman. At court she had been sensational and much admired by King Ferdinand who claimed to be 'in love with her beauty.' Queen Isabella swiftly arranged for Beatriz to be married and her husband was appointed Governor of the island of La Gomera in the Canary Islands. Isabella was in fact, consigning Beatriz to oblivion, banishing her forever, as the Canaries, at that time, were felt to be at the outer edge of the known world.

On his second voyage in 1493, Columbus and his ships were given a spectacular welcome at La Gomera. Feasting there was in abundance and fireworks, and general festivity: Beatriz was clearly pleased to have Columbus back. The story of their affair, mostly whispered of as 'secret', was revealed in a letter by Miguel de Cuneo, a childhood friend of Columbus, then one of his acquaintances. Unfortunately for Columbus, on a return journey some years later, he was devastated to find Beatriz had married again. She had an even more important husband this time and her title now was Lady of the Canaries. On that occasion Columbus stayed just long enough for his ships' supplies to be replenished—four days.

This may sound like an interesting little story and of no importance. But its outcome was far from little and very, very important. It changed the history of the world, of Africa, and of sugar. Beatriz gave Columbus cuttings of sugar-cane to take to the New World— and some of these he left in the West Indies. These islands, with their brilliant sunshine and plentiful supply of water, were perfectly suited for the growth and propagation of the plant. The sugar industry was about to explode.

In the Islamic medieval world, scientists had discovered how to crystallise and refine sugar, and mills were built in sugar-producing countries. The operation of these mills depended on wind and water and, of course, labour. The future of the islands was promising. (When the 'sugar-producing islands' were spoken of, people usually included Guiana which was not an island but a part of the South American mainland and very close to the islands.)

Before the industry took off, however, the supply of labour unexpectedly failed. The indigenous tribes had been expected to be trained to grow and harvest the cane but they quickly began to fall victim to the new diseases brought by Europeans and others from the old world. They had no resistance to these diseases and as a result their numbers were decimated.

This led to the beginning of the slave trade, which brought Africans in their thousands to labour in the islands. This new labour force was hardier and also expendable; slaves could be supplied in vast numbers. The plantations grew and expanded (they had to, the sugar-cane plants depleted the soil and there was no quick fix then), planters took their families to settle and grow rich, production was well organised and the profits rolled in.

Colonisation was well and truly established and would remain for centuries to follow.

Acknowledgements

This book has taken a long time to write—such a long time that many of the people to whom I owe so much, my older friends and my teachers, have sadly passed away. But they are thanked here, as are the other people who have helped me with their recalling of historical memories, their own memories and those of their antecedents, tales told, the precious books they didn't mind lending, the contacts they gave me, those contacts themselves—and, above all, their encouragement.

So much, so very much encouragement!

They are—Kathleen Herbert, Biddy Adamson, Desmond Fitz-Gerald, Yvonne Kensett, Lesley Theophilus, Lilli and Neville Armstrong, Elizabeth and Robert Druce, Mother Gonzaga O.S.U. from Ireland, Mother Magdalen Marryat O.S.U. (Trinidad) both nuns at the Ursuline Convent, in Georgetown, and Miss Florence McKinnon of Buxton Village, East Coast, Demerara, a story-teller without equal.

Special thanks go to the Great Cornard Writing Group, now defunct and, of course, the Bures Book Club, reading, meeting and discussing books for more than 20 years.

Members of The Kitchen, however transient, must also be thanked for their snippets of gossip, their tireless recounting of What the Old People Told Them about the Old Time Days before any of us were born—during 'what must have been a lonely childhood' people still tell me. (It wasn't.) And for filling my young days with such entertainment and spice....

My thanks to my parents, Adrianna and James Winter, for the childhood that I lived in the place that I lived.

Finally, my most grateful and lasting thanks go to David Helfrich for his tireless research into my family history, to Frank Lalljee for the introduction to David, to Roger Stokes for old photographs of Guiana he provided because mine were nowhere to be found, to Myrtle Chapman for unearthing many more old and hard-to-find photographs, and to Matthew Adamson for his practical, unceasing help, his invaluable advice and, above all, his encouragement.

PAM WALTERS

Demerara Sugar

Chapter One

Pagli mashed people and twisted their bones. Then she walked all over them in her bare feet. I used to listen for their screams.

It was obvious to a small child—I must have been about five—that there would be screams: Pagli was enormous. Huge feet, huge hands, huge body...

Huge, wicked, one-toothed grin.

No, no, they told me in The Kitchen, I'd got it all wrong. Pagli was a really good woman, there was not a wicked bone in her body. And why did I call her Pagli? That made her sound foreign, as though she came from abroad. But she lived right there on the very same sugar plantation as we did, born and lived there, and she was East Indian. They told me her correct name and how to say it. They stood over me and made me say it.

'Pagli,' I said.

'That's right,' they nodded, satisfied. 'Pagli.'

None of it made any sense to me, so I went on listening hopefully for the victim's screams that would liven up my afternoon rest. But the only sound that reached me in that two o'clock heat was the sleepy murmur of voices in The Kitchen.

They spoke highly of Pagli there. They had all undergone the same hideous twisting and mashing at her hands and they all swore by it. She didn't just twist them and mash them and walk all over them ... *she worked miracles.* They all felt like new people. Gone were their aches and pains, their niggles, gone their rheumatism, lumbago, arthritis—all, all had been crushed away by those powerful hands, mashed away by those feet under that massive body. You could always tell when someone in The Kitchen had been mashed by Pagli, the victim would turn up in the morning walking brisk-brisk and smelling hotly of Canadian Healing Oil.

They strongly recommended this torture to my mother who, to my alarm, took it seriously. 'A good mashing and twisting might do my poor bones the world of good,' I heard her say to Daddy. 'Old age is marching on, you know.' She was in her thirties; old age went on the march early in the tropics.

The day was always bright when I first saw it from behind the mosquito netting and my mother was always by the window doing her Deep Breathing exercises. She was a fan of Bernarr (BernaRR, please note, not Bernard) MacFadden, an American health-and-fitness guru in vogue at the time. He had written encyclopedias on health-and-fitness and his works were kept behind lock and key in the glass-fronted bookcase high on the wall in my parents' bedroom. (Later, I was to discover why the lock and key: the works were liberally illustrated with pictures of *naked people*. Not only illustrations, but in some cases *actual photographs*. Full frontal.) McFadden strongly recommended Deep Breathing.

'Blessed with another lovely day!' She'd say when she saw I was awake. My mother believed in counting her blessings as advised by the old hymn ('COUNT your BLESSINGS, count them ONE by ONE') and lovely days were a blessing, even though they were fairly common in British Guiana. There, the sun always shone and the sky was always blue, the wind always soft and warm. I'd hurry downstairs never doubting that not only was that day lovely, but every single day thereafter was going to be every bit as lovely.

Under-the-House, though, they were poised and waiting, ready to put these misconceptions right.

Under-the-House was not only a location, it was the Guianese equivalent of Below Stairs. It was also known as the Bottom-House. I was not allowed to use the word 'bottom' (it was said to be Rude) and it was reported when I did. 'Mistress!' The cry would go up. 'If you *hear* what Miss Pam say!'

The houses were built on pillars to protect them against flooding. This was no idle threat nor even just a possibility, but a very real danger in a country where the coastland had been reclaimed from the sea by the Dutch and a lot of it was still below sea level. Flooding was an even bigger danger on the sugar plantations.

We lived at Enmore, one of the plantations on the East

Coast, a place which had seen legendary floods. There was plenty of space under our elevated house for swings, a see-saw, tricycles and scooters and the ping pong table. A boat and oars were also kept high up on the rafters. There was Cookie the washerwoman with her tubs, while The Kitchen gathered for its meals Under-the-House.

Noon was the time they had what we called breakfast in the Colony. For The Kitchen, breakfast meant cook-up rice and salt-fish, door-stop chunks of bread and red margarine and great steaming enamel mugs of coffee. For me, this was the best part of the day.

Noon was the time I became invisible. I rode my tricycle slowly around and around, humming to myself while listening to the Kitchen gossip, filling my ears with all sorts of things a small child was not meant to hear. The Kitchen was supposed to have their meal in peace and I was not to bother them—humBUG was the word used, as in 'Don' humBUG a'we!'. But at noon all sorts of rules could be broken.

For my father rested then, directly above us in his Berbice chair in the gallery, legs out on the long arms of the planter's chair, the newspaper before him and a cold drink beside him, on a little tray which lay on the front legs of a stuffed alligator. (A hideous object, this. It sat upright, scaly tail swerved out behind it, its pale belly showing where it had been slit and stuffed, mouth wide open exhibiting fearsome teeth and an electric light bulb.) Noon was a sacred hour—an hour when no one, not even Woman Billy, nanny of my brother Bobby and me and guardian of my every waking moment—not even she dared raise her voice to tell me what not to do.

When my father left for the sugar factory I would be bidden upstairs for the afternoon rest. This was a sacred rite in the Colony, but only for ladies and little girls. Small boys like Bobby could get by with just playing quietly as long as they didn't disturb anyone. But before my rest there was noon and that heady hour of Kitchen gossip.

I could never hear enough of the disasters that had befallen everyone, or everyone they knew, or else were very soon going to befall them. These disasters were many and Mr. Motoo, the pedlar, kept us supplied with calamitous tales whenever he showed up. Going over and over them bit by bit—questioning them—laying them at the door of God and His will—blaming them on the devil, the Ole Higue, the mother-in-law or the next-door neighbour—all this caused a lot of agitated talk and gave a lot of pleasure to everyone. And by the end of the hour it always seemed that the day was never as lovely as my mother Upstairs had thought it was when I woke up, and there were no blessings to be counted. Not one.

According to those Under-the-House, the more glittering the sun … the more endlessly blue the sky … the more peaceful and quiet everything was in our little Colony … then the more likely it was that something **awful** would very soon happen.

'Something like what?' Goggle-eyed, I hungered for the hideous tales they were so good at telling. Tales that kept me awake in the black night, eyes looking beyond the blackness into even blacker corners. Nails bitten and bloody. It was no use brother Bobby, three years older than I, and very wise, say-ing, 'Oh, go to sleep will you, there's nothing there!' **I knew.**

'Ah, chile.' Heads shook, tones became sorrowful. 'Why you ask? Is why you want to know? What you know about life, eh? You is so young! So young and innocent! Pray God you never see the troubles we see! Pray God you never find out!'

But they told me all the same. Those skies, it seemed, could suddenly fill with rainclouds and flood *the entire Colony.* The fact that we lived below sea level was never far from anyone's mind. The rain would ruin the cane crops, bringing disease to the Colony and death to many. There would be even more mos-quitoes. Malaria killed. Typhoid fever killed. So did all those other diseases that had no name but were attributed to the will of God or the work of the devil and, who knew, perhaps even the mother-in-law. It had all happened before—the things they could tell you!—*and it could all happen again*.

On the other hand … those cloudless skies might remain forever blue … the sun go on burning … the earth parch and crack … the rivers dry up (ignore the fact that the word 'Gui-ana' was Aborigine for Land of Many Waters, that was only Ab-origine-talk and what did *they* know?) The fields of cane would wither and die. And then, of course, the whole Colony would die soon, very soon after. Sugar cane was, after all, the reason that we in the Colony lived, breathed and died.

Death was a favourite topic Under-the-House. Someone they knew had always just died. Each loved being first with the news, the howls of astonishment making it all worthwhile. 'Eh-eh! Is dead she dead? Man, you foolin' me! An' I see her just the other day looking so good and strong!'

Another much-loved topic was the doings of the Obe-ah-man. Obeah is the Guianese equivalent of African voodoo. It is said to have originated among the Ashanti in West Africa, and the word is a derivation of the Ashanti word Obayifo (said quickly—a long O then 'bay' pronounced as two syllables). The word means wizard. Obeah is a powerful supernatural force dedicated to doing evil and only evil. No one in Guiana ever doubted that it worked. No one doubted that the African slaves who had crossed an ocean with nothing—not even clothes on their backs—had brought with them a power as strange and terrible as this.

It was not widely practised, or so the colonial masters liked to think, but it was very widely discussed. There was a hideous tale of a little English girl who was kidnapped then slaughtered by the Obeah-man and her eye pinned under her father's ta-ble—the dining-table, according to The Kitchen, right on the floor-bell which he used to summon the next course at din-ner. (Mr. Motoo, the pedlar, had vouched for this.) When the Englishman looked to see what his foot had squelched on, he found it was his daughter's eye … and all because he was go-ing to sack someone. It just went to show, the White-man had to think hard before he went about sacking people. Sacking people did no one any good, and certainly not this particular White-man. That, at any rate, was the way they told it.

Their favourite story was the one about a young girl who died in her sleep and was buried … but when the coffin was lat-er opened (her mother having had a Premonition) they found that she hadn't been dead at all, she'd been buried alive, and the coffin was opened *just in time*. I'd toss and turn in my bed at night, terrified to fall asleep in case I died, and wondering if my mother could be trusted to have a Premonition.

The first person I knew who died was Jamesie Jones. He was the plantation's carpenter and coffin maker. We could see his house and workshop some distance from ours and if the air was still we could hear the hammer blows as he worked away at his coffin-making. I always knew when he was making one because the whole Kitchen would clap their hands over their ears and moan when the hammering started. 'Oh GAWD—*is who turn next! I ask you, is who turn!*'

Jamesie Jones sometimes passed the back of our house, businesslike and purposeful, never pausing to gossip or pass time with anyone. There was no doubt that he looked good and strong, a tall black man always in khaki shirt and trousers, with a khaki-coloured fedora hat which he lifted to all the women. Once, I was watching him go by from an upstairs window when he glanced up. I was too little to see over the sill and did so only by pulling myself up, taking a quick look, then falling back. He could have seen no part of me, only the huge bow on my head bobbing up and down, but he stopped and did an unforgettable thing. He lifted his hat to it.

One night it rained suddenly, so the story went, and Jamesie Jones got out of bed to close the windows and was soaked to the skin. He caught a chill and was dead the next day. I heard Aunt Vic telling it to The Kitchen with all the frills, in that way she had of telling things that made you think she'd actually been there. I stole away and stood at the window, peering out at Jamesie Jones's house in the distance and thinking about him being dead. Then I heard the hammer blows. Heard them clearly.

Someone was making a coffin!

Aunt Vic was wrong! They were all wrong! How could he be dead? Someone was making a coffin…. Only Jamesie Jones made coffins! I could hear his hammer distinctly. I rushed back toThe Kitchen shouting the good news. 'Listen! I can hear Jamesie Jones! He's not dead, he's making a coffin! I can hear his hammer! Listen!'

There was a terrible silence. They turned to look at me, eyes huge, faces aghast. The hammer blows were clear.

'Is he own coffin they mekkin'!' Someone moaned. 'The chile hear them mekkin' Jamesie Jones' coffin!'

A hand seized me and I was hustled upstairs for yet another rest. Behind me, madness broke out.

Shortly after that, someone saw an Ole Higue.

In my mind, Ole Higues were vaguely associated with witches, the kind seen in my Snow White story book. If they were different at all then perhaps it was because their skins were black. Woman Billy had threatened once—but once only—that if I didn't behave the Ole Higue would come and get me.

My mother had swiftly put a stop to that. The Ole Higue never came and I lost interest. Everyone knew there were no such things as witches, I was assured, neither black nor white, and as for Ole Higues—! (Much laughter.) If Woman Billy was not aware of this, it was simply because poor Woman Billy had had no Advantages. I was to forget it, forget all that silly talk. The Ole Higue would never come even if it did exist, which it did not.

It came early one morning. Or rather, news of its coming did. I woke to a commotion, feet running up the back steps and around The Kitchen, voices high-pitched and frenzied, my mother standing over me quietly to make sure I was asleep. I kept my eyes closed. She threw on a kimono (it was the era of glamorous Chinese kimonos, all Guianese ladies seemed to float about in them) and rushed downstairs. I tiptoed down soon after and listened outside the swing doors that led toThe Kitchen. No one seemed to notice my feet which must have shown clearly under them.

'The woman was walking down the road—jus' walking down the road I tell you, like anybody coulda been doing! Like you or me coulda been doing … jus walking—'

'Go on! What happen to the woman?'

'What happen! Oh GAWD! It wasn't even a dark night! Clear enough so she could see—and she see this pile a' thing that look like old clothes lying there. What tell she to pick it up—**what tell she!**'

Gasps … a single moan … horror straining at the leash, waiting to let rip.…

'What it was, Ruby? What she pick up?'

'Tell we, tell we!'

'What she pick up? **Was the Ole Higue skin!**'

I had not known about this. I had not known that Ole Higues had this advantage over ordinary witches—that they could not be identified because **they took their skins off.** That meant anyone could be an Ole Higue. **Anyone.** Any one of the women in The Kitchen, even Woman Billy, screeching along with the rest of them.

'She din realize at first! How anybody to know? She know it feel funny, not like clothes feel … more like chicken-skin. Then when she realize what she holding, she drop it quick-quick! But she too late!'

Too late!

The Ole Higue had come at her out of the sky, flapping like a monster cockerel, with hellish squawking—it wrapped its skinless bloody shape around her, sank its teeth into her breast and gulped her blood with horrid sucking noises. Then it left (taking its skin with it) and the woman staggered half-conscious to her home, covered with its blood, dripping. When she suddenly appeared at the door, reeling, bloody and jabbering, her horrified family thought she was an Ole Higue herself.

'**Is me! Is me!**' She kept shrieking. The screaming went on and on.

They stripped her and washed her under the standpipe, thinking that she'd been knifed by some madman. But when every last drop of blood had been washed away, there was not a slash to be found. Not a cut, not a scratch, not a bruise. Only the teeth-marks of the Ole Higue where she'd sucked and gulped (presumably all that blood lost in ripping off the skin had to be replaced).

Now the woman lay on her bed and stared at something no one could see. Gibbered. She would be taken to the hospital that day, perhaps was there this very minute, but nothing could be done for her. They all knew that. They all knew what would happen to her.

Now she too would become an Ole Higue.

I crept upstairs.

The Ole Higue came for me that night.

I saw it flying high across the sky on a giant pointer-broom, its blood streaking redly behind it. Watched it halt in flight outlined against the moon—saw it turn and head straight for our house. I knew that it was coming for me. I could do nothing. I could not run, could not move, could not call out. It flew straight through the window, right through the mosquito netting and wrapped its dripping ghastliness all around me.

I screamed and screamed and could not stop screaming.

When my parents rushed in the Ole Higue had vanished. Not a drop of blood was left behind, not a tooth mark. Not a single piece of pointer-broom. No ripped mosquito netting. Only me, a wide-eyed child who **knew** what she had seen.

I could convince neither parent. I couldn't even convince Bobby who stood by the bedroom door really wanting to believe. Their voices were soothing, their presence reassuring. Little girls should not listen behind doors, they said, they should not listen to things that were meant for grown-up ears only. When they did, they had nightmares, so let it be a lesson to me. That was all it was. A nightmare.

Then I saw it, the proof. Blood. A drop of blood on my foot. 'A mosquito,' my mother said, 'They get through the net, you know they do.' And she wiped the blood away swiftly. But I glanced up and saw the look on her face.

I am still trying to forget it.

It was after this visitation that the edict went out: only good things must be spoken of when the child was around. **Uplifting** things. I had what was called a Wild Imagination. I wasn't sure what that was but it was obviously worse than having malaria. It was bad enough, my mother kept saying, having to bring children up in a place like that, there was no need to expose them unnecessarily to things they shouldn't hear or see.

Until now it seemed to have been generally assumed by both those Upstairs and those Under-the-House, that a child of my age wouldn't understand what was being said. Whether it was the gist of the conversation I was not expected to grasp or the language it was spoken in, I am not sure.

The Guianese tongue, more so when spoken in the country

areas, can be difficult to understand even when you are growing up with it. The Kitchen spoke perfectly comprehensible English when they wished to be understood, an English spiced with splendid old-fashioned words and phrases that stopped newcomers to the Colony in their tracks. These were words and phrases that slaves had picked up from their colonial masters in days long gone and passed down the years. When the descendants of those slaves didn't want to be understood they would lapse into a baffling jargon that went as far back as the beginning of slavery.

African slaves newly arrived in the Colony would have been seized from different tribes and spoke different dialects so they had no language in common. They picked up a primitive type of English from the worst possible teachers: from the slaves who preceded them, who in turn had done their picking up from the plantation overseers. At that time, overseers were recruited mostly from the dregs of English society and spoke the language badly themselves. The slaves also learned from the missionaries who read the Bible to them in a sing-song biblical style, rather like Welsh-speak, which they quickly imitated, a style that has remained.

To add to the confusion, the Colony passed from one nation to another, from Dutch to English. There was a later influx of French and Portuguese, Maltese and East Indians, who came as indentured labour. Babel must have sounded very much like it. East Indians in particular can be incomprehensible. In the country districts there were whole pockets of them who, generation after generation, made no effort (or pretended to make no effort, it could never be certain which) to learn English.

Woman Billy had been engaged to look after Bobby and me because, among other things, she Spoke Well. Now, she was also to make sure that I did not hear and see that which I should not. The number of things I was not to hear and see appeared to be legion. It was all right for Bobby to hear and see things, everyone knew he was a sensible child, level-headed and reasoning, the kind of child who could take Ole Higues or leave them alone. He was being brought up like a man, exposure to the things of the world was good for him.

I was to be a little lady. The world was to be vetted and censored. If necessary, it was to be kept from me and I from it.

The happy hour with The Kitchen ceased. During their breakfast hour I lay in a hammock on the verandah with crayons and colouring books, longing to hear more about the Obeah-man and the little girl who had fallen through the hole in the latrine and been drowned. Not daring to think about the Ole Higue. Dreaming of the Fair Maids who could not possibly be evil, as people said, how could they be with a name like that? Wondering what fresh disaster Mr. Motoo, the pedlar, would have to report and would I ever hear about it....

The news was broadcast at six o'clock on the radio, after which it was hastily switched off by some adult hand. Not before snatches of a mournful dirge were heard though, something else I was not supposed to hear. This sad tune was a prelude to the Death Announcements, necessarily broadcast by radio in that hot climate, in those days of swift, necessary, same-day burial.

'Why are you switching it off? It could be someone we know!'

I used to worry.

'All the more reason you don't want to hear about it, chile,' I'd be told.

Chapter Two

When my mother referred despairingly to 'a place like that' everyone knew she meant Enmore. It was one of the sugar plantations strung along the east coast of Demerara which, in turn, was one of Guiana's three counties. Enmore belonged, like most of the plantations, to Bookers Brothers McConnell & Co. Ltd., the firm responsible for the largest part of the Colony's sugar output.

Bookers had its start in 1815. That was the year a quite extraordinary young man called Josias Booker went out to Guiana to manage one of the sugar plantations. Extraordinary because on arriving in the Colony he saw only the advantages—they were few—of his new position, and seemed to have ignored the drawbacks, which were considerably more. Right away he started urging those of his relatives who would pay any attention, to join him. The Booker clan must have been just as extraordinary as Josias for some of them did indeed join their young relative—in spite of the heat, the sickness and malaria, the discontent and uprisings among the slaves, and the other myriad discomforts affecting Guiana then. Like Josias, they seemed to ignore all these. They had gone out there to prosper, and they just went right ahead and prospered.

After the abolition of slavery, when plantations were being sold at giveaway prices, the Booker family moved in and bought them. The firm grew enormously and became so powerful that by the1930s British Guiana was known laughingly throughout the Caribbean as Bookers Guiana. Josias Booker left his mark. In spite of his living in Guiana for only seven years, the name Booker is still prominent there and in the City of London.

Enmore was reached from Georgetown by the East Coast Road. This dispiriting highway wound along the coastline through long stretches of uncultivated land ... through paddy-fields, through coconut palms, through sad, straggling villages. Bright signs in these villages urged the inhabitants to drink Vimto or Coca-Cola and to use Thermogene Medicated Rub. Music blared away on loudspeakers to an invisible population. Drainage ditches ran alongside the road, not always draining but always smelling vilely.

There was no way that even the sharpest observer could have guessed that inland—just a few miles inland, to the right of that dreary road—lay the vast acres that were the life—the blood—the beating heart of Guiana.

The sugar plantations.

Lusignan, Cane Grove, Paradise, Rose Hall. Nonpareil. Sophia. Bachelor's Adventure—!

They had romantic names. Names to tease the imagination, to ask about, to listen to long sad tales about. Tales of people who had lived quiet lives only to be hacked to bits by rebelling slaves or be shot through the head by a jealous lover. Names to make up stories about if no one had any to tell. Enmore had an uninspiring name, just a place in England, or it may have been Scotland, that someone had come from. I could make up nothing romantic about it. It has disappointed me all my life.

My mother had grown up there. My grandmother lived there in a small house on a large piece of land, with guinea fowl, an earth oven, and that most fascinating of buildings to a child, an outside latrine perched over the water. It was only a mile or so from our house but to me it was truly another world.

The people who went by the Compound where the staff lived did so with purpose. They were either maintenance men looking after the upkeep of the houses, or gardeners who looked after the grounds, or people who worked in the kitchens. Those were the people who passed by our house. The people who passed by my grandmother's house were different. Sometimes they had purpose, sometimes they had not. Sometimes their skins were white.

They were the descendants of the indentured labourers who had taken the place of the African slaves after Abolition.

Indentured labour was the brainchild of Sir John Gladstone (father of the future Prime Minister William Gladstone), who owned sugar plantations in Guiana. Portuguese, Chinese and Maltese labourers were used initially, and it was the descendants of these who now ran shops and other small businesses on the sugar estates and in Georgetown. They were very successful shopkeepers and business people but as labourers in the cane fields they were not. They were people who had been born and lived in different climates and were not used to the heat. They could not work in it, they sickened and died in their droves.

The East Indians (from Uttar Pradesh, hence *East* Indians) came from a similar climate to Guiana and could work all day under that fierce Demerara sun.

In theory they went to Guiana under contract, to work for an agreed number of years with the promise of a free return voyage to India when those years were done. The agents who contracted them painted glowing pictures: advancement in the workplace and up the social scale, perhaps in government even. (That happened, of course, but it took generations.) Many expected to send for their families, or to return with riches.

Most stayed forever.

They were indentured labour and they did the work that the slaves had done. They were fed as the slaves had been fed. They were housed in the same one-room dwellings as the slaves. They were treated like slaves.

They were even called slaves.

I can remember hearing them referred to as 'indentured slaves'. The plantocracy, having been always surrounded by slaves, had 'slavery' stamped indelibly on their psyche.

As a small child I was already vaguely aware that any socializing with the estate children, or any lengthy exchange of words, was a no-no. It simply wasn't done. I longed for conversations with little girls my age and to know about them and how they lived. How many brothers and sisters did they have? What did they do in school? What did they eat at home, did they really have curry and roti every day? We had curry only on high days and holidays, and when my parents had an informal lunch party. Or, best of all, when the meat from town ('The Meat Company') was off and there were only 'provisions' (ground crops). What a curry sauce could do for boring English Potatoes I still find miraculous.

So I had no enlightening conversations with children on the plantation and I did not know how they lived. I had never seen a range-dwelling, which was where they lived, and I knew nothing about them apart from the name.

It was the fact that they all lived in one room that ruled out conversation. Little girls who lived in one-room dwellings knew and saw things they should not know and see. Not only about life and death but about conception and birth. They would have seen their grandparents die, perhaps horribly or happily. They would have seen and heard their younger siblings being conceived and born.

They knew about wife-beatings and wife-cuttings (with a cutlass) and nose-bobbings (this last for infidelity, suspected, reported or real). They knew about murder.

'These are things little girls like you should not know about,' Woman Billy told me sternly, when persistently questioned.

'What about little boys?' I asked. Bobby was sometimes allowed to play cricket with a small, select group of boys on the plantation.

'Little boys born knowing these things,' I was told, 'It don' matter 'bout Master Bobby, he got sense.' Unlike you, she did not add. This was something I was to hear again and again.

I was full of questions. These never seemed to get answers and my questions were always treated as Eye-Pass.

Eye-Pass is peculiar to Guiana. Disrespect—rudeness—anything at which adults chose to take umbrage or, as in this case, simply asking a question grown-ups find awkward to answer—all this and more is deemed Eye-Pass.

'Chile, you mek yo' eye-pass yo' Grandmother!'

'What you want to know bout these things for? Is Big-People business, is nothing to do with you!'

When questioned my mother just looked at me, amused. I was frequently hearing that children should be seen and not heard.

I thought about it when alone in the silent hours of the afternoon, the hot hours when the house slept. I sat with my chin on my knees in a huge wicker chair in the gallery, the garden fragrant outside, cool ferns cascading from huge brass urns around me. ('What the chile doin' hunch up in the big chair?') I thought about slavery and all the other things connected with it, things which had surrounded me all my life but which were so suddenly new to me.

I was at school by then, old enough to take books down from the shelves and to find the subjects I wanted to know about. To read how other people's great-grandparents had come to the Colony, how they had lived and died.

The East Indians were the fortunate ones. Called East Indians because they were from the east of India, and also to identify them from West Indians and Amerindians, the indentured labour from those parts brought their families and possessions; they came because they wanted to. They travelled hopefully.

The others—those who came on slave ships from Africa—brought nothing. I pictured the scene, hunched in the wicker chair in the silence and heat … they would be tending their maize plot, or fishing, perhaps washing clothes by the river, the women calling to each other or their children, not far from the village. The steady thump-thump of the giant mortar-and-pestle they used to pound the maize would be echoing through the forest, as much a background noise as the flowing water and the birdsong. Then—silence.

Sometimes, they knew what that silence meant. When they did, they turned and fled, they kept on fleeing. Those who did not know—those who went back to find out what it was all about—found themselves in the dark holds of ships, flesh piled on flesh, vomiting, defecating, dying, decomposing, travelling across an ocean to slavery. Sometimes they never arrived.

The slave trade did not stop with the Abolition in 1833. It was risible to think that a trade so lucrative and so widespread would come to a halt simply because an Act had been passed far away in a place called Parliament. It carried on briskly, the slave ships doing a surface trade as legitimate merchantmen, plying between Africa and the Colonies, their stinking holds stuffed to overflowing with black treasure. When a ship of the King's navy was sighted, for the seas were patrolled as well as they could be to see that the new law was upheld—the incriminating evidence was rapidly disposed of. Weighted down in groups, the black gold was flung overboard. The sea would be calm, the sharks would have done their work, the bloody sea would be far behind them by the time the patrol ship arrived.

So they had travelled to Guiana. So they had lived and died, the forebears of the people around me. People who passed by every day—came up the back steps carrying wood and water—who worked in The Kitchen and the garden. People I knew.

This new realisation was overwhelming and threatened to take over all my thinking. Always a solemn child, I would stand at The Kitchen door and gaze big-eyed at each one of them in turn, wondering. They found this disquieting.

'Eh-eh! But what humBUG the chile!'

I tried to ask them about their great-grandparents and beyond but was not taken seriously.

'But look botheration!'

'Chile, is humBUG you humBUGging a'we!'

Finally, I was told firmly that if I had nothing better to do then I must **keep out of The Kitchen.**

My own father went to Enmore as an overseer. These young men supervised the Indian and African labourers in the cane fields and were predominantly English, Irish and Scots, with some Guianese. Bachelors mainly, they had a well-earned reputation for roistering. They lived in the Overseers' Quarters, narrow, range-like buildings on pillars, buildings which were no more than a row of bedrooms and showers with a long, enclosed passageway at the side.

Each overseer had his own houseboy. Sometimes when on an economy drive, two of them would share a boy. A houseboy who could cook rice and saltfish and boil English potatoes was deemed to be employable. He also served up tinned sardines with a dash of pepper-sauce, fried corned beef and mashed potatoes and, if he wanted his life to be worth living, he quickly learned the recipe for rum swizzle and how to shake it with panache. A really enterprising houseboy would supplement this fare with curries cooked by his mother, at a price. An overseer who didn't like curry was a thin man.

Cooking was done in the open air on a coal-pot under the

Quarters and meals were taken in the Mess. The boys were supposed to use their masters' supplies only, and these were kept in mesh safes in the overseers' rooms, the safe legs standing in water-filled tins with paraffin added, supposedly to discourage the ants. Houseboys were forbidden to beg, borrow or steal from each other. Begging and borrowing was rife all the same, and stealing flourished: one houseboy even gave his name to a prospective employer as You Sonofagun. Some were very good at their jobs and could, if necessary, wash and iron as well as any of the washerwomen, although they had more sense than to do so. The washerwomen depended on the Quarters for their living and ran an efficient laundry service, taking their particular overseer's washing away twice a week (or more often if he didn't own many clothes) and returning them stone-washed, starched and ironed, on a wooden tray carried on their heads. This was all covered with a piece of netting to protect it from the dirt and dust. (This puzzled me as a small child—surely the dirt and dust could get through a piece of netting just as easily as the mosquitoes did?) The washerwomen were known to hurl a mean stone at houseboys who were seen to wash and hang out anything more than a tea-towel. 'Is tek you tekkin the food from m'children mouth! Don' lemme me see you on a dark night!"

Overseeing was a lonely life for young men. They worked, they read, and they roistered. Some took an interest in wildlife, although the Company frowned on the keeping of snakes, tarantulas, alligators and similar domestic pets and the houseboys were not supportive in these activities. They preferred to provide female company—for a fee—and paraded young girls—sometimes very young girls—for their masters' pleasure. Soft-eyed, sari-clad girls, all called, it seemed, Babsi or Baby, the latter an off-putting name.

Sometimes (having first obtained permission from the Company) an overseer would return from home leave in England with a wife. A young, fresh, blooming wife, pink-cheeked, bright-eyed with shining hair. The couple would be given a bungalow, acquire furniture and servants. Then the loneliness … the unvarying routine of the days … the lack of like-minded female companionship ... the flat monotony of the land around her, all would begin to hack away and erode her personality. The new wife would have brought with her few of the inner resources so vital to making a success of life on a sugar plantation in what was readily admitted to be one of the more backward British colonies.

Her style of cooking, if she had one, would be far removed from that of her kitchen. The local produce would be viewed with dismay if not downright disgust. She would not have the interest in clothes that the Guianese women had and, being the wife of an overseer, would not have had the money to employ one of the very talented and inexpensive Workers (dressmakers in Guiana were mysteriously called Workers) to sew for her. The light crepe de chine and Liberty lawn dresses so suitable for the few warm days of English summer could not survive the pounding and beating and rubbing with Gossages Brown Soap that they got in the washerwoman's tub. They quickly perished in the searing sun that dried them.

No doubt the new wife could knit beautifully, as all Englishwomen could then, but knitting as a time-killer soon proved impossible in that heat. Within months the vivid young bride would become wispy and faded and people would wonder aloud what on earth Good Old So-and-So who used to be able to drink you under the table, could ever have seen in her. While she ... she went from window to window in her bungalow each morning, watching for the slow return of the estate dray-cart from the station, bringing the mail from England. Sometimes.

In happy contrast, there were a few new wives who would have read everything that was printed about the Colony before they arrived there, who were fascinated by the many peoples and their culture and eager to learn more about them, who were ecstatic about the brightly-coloured flowers and fruit and wasted no time in organizing a garden and growing their own, who wanted to learn how to cook curry and rice and local produce—and soon did it better than their cooks. But of those there were only a few. They could be recognised in the market wearing a large hat and carrying a large basket, accompanied by their cook, also carrying a large basket and wearing a smaller hat, surrounded by market women instructing the new madam on how to cook the produce. There were few sightings of a white woman in the market in those days and the sellers sat up and took notice, so they would be noticed too and remembered. They enquired at length about the lady's health, about her husband's health and offered her their best recipes.

Later, the need for social life on the plantations was recognized. Clubhouses were built, with libraries, dance floors, and tennis courts. Station-wagons ferried wives and families to town and to other plantations for tea, drinks, and tennis parties. Marriages were made and flourished. The most successful marriages, it must be said, were those made with local girls from Georgetown families. These girls, who were invariably very good-looking, had of course a wide social circle which happily absorbed their overseer husbands and their friends. (Interestingly, these local wives and their families had to be vetted by the Management and permission given!) Above all the local girls had jobs and interests of their own and spent no time looking out of the window for the dray cart.

All these changes happened after the Second World War. Before the First War and between the Wars, a woman's days on the sugar plantations slipped by unnoticed. Sometimes, they and she could both be gone and no one noticed.

The overseers' work took them to Back-dam, the cane fields worked by East Indian and Negro labourers. A network of canals ran through the fields, where giant mules on the bank pulled huge punts loaded with cane to the factory. The overseers all rode mules, expensive beasts bought from other lands and held to be more precious than the young men themselves. The first question asked when a riding accident was reported was 'But the mule—is the mule all right?' The overseer and his mule were followed aback by a mule-boy who travelled on foot with his master's lunch. He tended the mule when the overseer dismounted and kept it watered, making sure the expensive animal did not take to its heels.

My Grandmother's house, lying some distance back from that long straight road that led out of the plantation, was a haven of rattan chairs, cool breezes and good cooking for James, my father, and his friend Charles when their day aback was over. Grandmother (called Mother by her children and grandchildren, which to this day causes confusion) had four daughters, grandly named Rebecca, Adrianna, Victorene and Sybille. They came to be known, as everyone but Mother could have told they would be known, as Bec, Ad, Vic and Syb.

'We had a quiet courtship, your father and I,' my mother told me when I was deemed sufficiently mature to talk to about such things.

'Where did you go? What did you do?' To me, courtship meant wide stone terraces with cracked urns, roses tumbling from sun-warmed English walls, the evening air heavy with their scent. A pale moon loitering. A single star. I had read a book called *The Rosary* where couples courted in similar surroundings, and my mother often sang a song of the same name, accompanying herself on the piano.

'Go?' She looked surprised. 'Do? Where was there to go? What was there to do? We were **here**, remember, in this place, on this very plantation. I was living in Mother's house. There was nowhere to go, nothing to do.'

'No—no Clubhouse?'

The Clubhouse had been built when I was about six. It had a dining-room, a bar with a billiard table and a library full of Dorothy L. Sayers and Edgar Wallace mysteries. It was a place for overseers to take guests, when they had any, or just to spend an evening.

'Gracious me, no. There was nothing before the Clubhouse. People played cards in the evening, or read, or went to bed early. James and I sat on the rattan chairs in Mother's living-room. We talked.'

I knew the chairs well. My Grandmother had bought them when her four daughters grew up, presumably for just this purpose.

'You—you just sat there? **Talked?**' This bore no semblance to the courtships in the books I'd read.

'We sat in peace and total understanding.'

She seemed miffed at my own total lack of understanding.

'Being together, being in each other's company, hearing each other's voices, exploring each other's minds, that was enough,' She tried to explain. But it was many, many years before that explanation made any sense to me.

'And then—?'

There had to be more!

'Then when it was time for James to leave I went with him as far as the main road. The Company road. When he got half-way down the road he turned and waved, and I waved back.'

I could say nothing. I just sat there and looked at her.

'I told you,' she said at last, 'We had a quiet courtship.'

What I didn't learn until later was that back at the house all hell would have broken loose. What did Mr. Winter **mean**, Rebecca wanted to know, by coming every evening and sitting on the rattan chairs? What was he **up** to? Had he **said** anything to Mother? If not, then why didn't Mother **do** something? How much longer was this to be allowed to **go on?**

'As long as it takes,' was Mother's answer.

I have no record of how long it took, but two years is what has stuck in my mind. They were married on the 16th of October in 1918, the date is engraved on the napkin rings they were given as wedding presents. There was a picture of Adrianna on her wedding day, the band of her veil low on her forehead, her waistline also low. It is a happy thought that fashion had not by-passed even A Place Like That.

It is disturbing, though, to realize that I know so little of my father's life before he went to Enmore. It wasn't that I didn't ask—I asked repeatedly. It was simply that I was never told.

Guianese, for reasons known only to themselves and God, preferred to keep the past hidden. Shrouded, never spoken of, at least not to children. Children's questions were answered by a broadside of adult questions.

'Child, what you want to know **for?**'

'Why you don' mind yo' own business?'

'Why you asking **now?** You know how long ago that happen?'

Or—the ultimate put-down—'Child, is make you making yo' eyes pass me!' Eye-Pass being, of course, the unforgivable crime. Even more unforgivable than the crime was the fact that the child seldom knew when it was being committed. Anything at which an adult chose to take umbrage was Eye-Pass.

My own mother never needed to use any of these answers. A swift stiffening of the back—a shake of the head followed by a stern look through steel-rimmed glasses—and I knew that I was treading on forbidden ground.

Why it should have been forbidden is still unclear.

This has been much discussed among my contemporaries who met with the same responses. Theories abound. One thought is that the early colonists, the settlers and the slaves— the slaves in particular—had to put the past behind them, to put aside the memories of the places and the families they had left, simply to make life in a new country tolerable.

Another more obvious theory, and probably the main reason, is that to our parents and grandparents, and their parents, so many things were held to be shameful. A downturn in fortune was always shaming. Unavoidable external influences may have caused that downturn, but it was still shaming. Drunkeness—daytime drunkeness—was shaming, it being permitted between the hours of 6 p.m. and 6 a.m. only. Illegitimacy, if known, was shaming—this, in a country where Outside (common-law) wives and Outside children existed in their swarms. Being Taken-In when a child appears to have been shaming.

Taking-In was fairly common in Guiana. If there were more children in a family than the parents could afford to keep, better-off relatives or friends would Take-in the child of their choice. Sometimes this was an excellent move for the child, who might then be better clothed, fed and educated than its siblings, sometimes going to private schools. The gap between the siblings would be marked, often unbridgeable.

Frequently the opposite happened and the child took up the position of Household Drudge. Guianese kitchens were full of Drudges—penniless spinsters, young unmarried mothers whose babies had themselves been Taken-in, and near-invisible wispy women with dead faces whose histories of Taking-in were long forgotten.

My father and his two sisters, Marie and Lily, had been adopted when their father died of a fever on the Demerara River and was buried on its banks by Aborigines. The adoptive parents were an aunt and uncle, their father's brother and his American wife, so the children remained within the family circle. All the same, the shadow of Taking-in seems to have hovered over the adoption. Perhaps that was why it was never spoken of.

Or perhaps it was because their mother who was, in fact, East Indian, let them go. Maybe that was the shameful thing. She must have felt, when her husband died so young, that it would be better for her children to be brought up by their relatives in a complete family, one with a man in the house. Or maybe she couldn't afford to bring them up herself … although, when she died, she left a house to my mother, a large house in a busy village, with a garden of tropical fruit. Whatever the reason, no one spoke of it. The conversation was always quite deliberately changed.

Nor did anyone speak of her in later years. Even now, when I know so much more of my family history, I know nothing about my paternal grandmother.

Had it not been for the Great-Aunts, the family history would now be forgotten. The old ladies, three of them, lived in a dark old house in Georgetown. I have a memory that is barely that … a picture that wavers and never settles into place … of old lace and wrinkled skin, gnarled fingers gripped around the head of a stick. The smell of camphor and beeswax, and darkness everywhere.

The Venetian blinds in the Great-Aunts' house were never raised, I was told, the sun was never allowed in. This I learned from those Under-the-House, who seemed to know everything about the old ladies even though they themselves had never been to Georgetown, let alone to the Great-Aunts' house.

'Why not?' It was an unthinkable feat, to keep that sun out.

'Because of their skins,' was the mystifying answer, 'And the mahogany furniture.'

It was some time before I understood that white women in Guiana were said to live in this underwater gloom to keep their skins white and the mahogany furniture dark.

Chapter Three

The Kitchen got their inside knowledge of the Great-Aunts and their domestic arrangements from Mr. Motoo, the pedlar, who in turn claimed to have been patronised by them for years. This is unlikely. The Misses Winter were not the sort of people who bought from pedlars. Their father had kept them supplied with silks and muslins from far-off places, bales enough to last them a lifetime, an advantage few colonials would have had. Not only that—the Misses Winter considered themselves a cut above most Georgetown ladies, for **they** had been born Abroad. They counted among their antecedents Sir James Spearman Winter, once Attorney-General of Newfoundland.

They would not have countenanced allowing their household to chat and gossip with a pedlar Under the House. 'Countenanced' was the sort of word the Misses Winter would have used.

The family had come to Guiana from Newfoundland. They had been traders there and some continued to trade, while some took to the bush, prospecting for gold and diamonds and acquiring aborigine women and illegitimate ('Outside') children along the way. (This was never spoken of by the family. When Mr. Motoo and The Kitchen discussed it they used lowered tones with many glances over their shoulders at the little girl (me) circling on her tricycle. There was much muttering about Little Ears.)

Fortunately, Great-Aunt Bessie loved talking about the family. In that time that my memory of her began, those days when I was very young and she was very old, she used to talk at length to the younger family members, the older ones no doubt having heard all her tales. My cousin Kathleen was already a teenager then, responsive and bright and definitely Aunt Bessie's favourite. Biddy, Kathleen's sister, was much younger, and I was simply the even younger little cousin who tagged along. But young as Biddy and I were, we were already avid readers and listeners, eager to hear those accounts of the faraway countries and distant days Aunt Bessie had known, and we were full of questions that were actually **answered**. Aunt Bessie seemed not to have heard of Eye-Pass. If she had, she had long dismissed it as just another Guianese custom with which she would have nothing to do.

There were many, many tales. Anecdotes about life in Newfoundland—schooldays in England—and growing up in what was to young Bessie the strange and inhospitable colony of Guiana. I was not aware as I listened that memories were being made even then. For my most vivid memory of Great-Aunt Bessie was the day we unpacked The Wardrobe. My two older cousins did it all, Aunt Bessie was too old and frail to take part and I was too small to do anything but keep out of the way.

That day there was an air of purpose about her as she issued crisp instructions to her young nieces, instructions that left us bug-eyed and wordless.

'Today,' she said, 'We will unpack The Wardrobe.'

None of us could believe we had heard what we had heard. '?-?-?'

'It is time—today we will unpack The Wardrobe.'

'!-!-!'

We were transfixed. Our Great-Aunt was proposing to begin a task that had been talked about often but put off many times. Our eyes swivelled from the old lady to The Wardrobe.

Never once in living memory had it been opened. Never once had any member of the family seen behind its locked doors. Now we—we, the youngest!—were going to unpack the Wardrobe!

It is impossible to think of The Wardrobe in anything but Capital Letters. The Bed rated the same respect because of its size and intricately carved posts and headboard but, maybe because it was in everyday use, to us it was just an imposing piece of furniture. But—The Wardrobe—!

That was Pandora's Box ... the pirate's treasure chest ... anything that a child's imagination wanted it to be. Wherever she had lived it had dominated Great-Aunt Bessie's bedroom, had kept children's eyes rivetted to it—kept the household whispering, wondering. It towered almost to the ceiling, its doors securely locked, the key dangling with the other household keys from the ring at the old lady's waist. The Wardrobe had been part of the furnishings of her parents' home along with the massive Bed, all travelling with them across the sea from Newfoundland to Guiana, and no matter to what rented house Aunt Bessie moved these two things always went with her.

The Great-Aunts were proud of the fact that they were not Guianese. They pointed it out at every opportunity. ('Guianese? No, not we. We were born abroad.') They had all three been born in St. John's, Newfoundland, Elizabeth Winter (Bessie), Bella (Arabella) and Mary. (And there was, of course, that distinguished gentleman, Sir James Spearman Winter, once Attorney General of Newfoundland, always in the background.)

When I first knew Aunt Bessie, already a very old lady, she lived in a tiny house tucked away among very large ones. She was small and imperious and wore grey dresses down to her ankles, with her hair in a bun on the top of her head.

The house was quite close to the Sea Wall. All her life she had insisted on living near the sea, and not far from where her father had built his home when he first brought his family to British Guiana—that solitary pink spot on the map of South America, part of the British Empire on which no one ever dreamed that the sun would one day set.

Great-Aunt Bessie was fond of recounting that an ancestor from Devon, England, had been given a grant of land in Newfoundland for services rendered to the Crown in one of its many wars (she never mentioned which). Settled in the new world, he and his offspring built up a thriving business shipping cod from Newfoundland to the West Indies and British Guiana, where salt-fish was the staple diet of the slaves and labourers on the plantations. The ships returned with sugar and molasses and, of course, casks of rum.

Bessie was nine years old when she and her sisters sailed from St. John's. Her father switched his business from Water Street, St. John's to Water Street, Georgetown, built himself a fine home close to the Sea Wall, named it 'Avalon' in a fit of nostalgia, and raised his large family of five boys and three girls. Nothing is known of his wife apart from the fact that she was prolific. He made his contribution to the civic life of the town by serving a term as mayor.

Sugar was doing well on the world markets and the Grand Banks were still full of cod, so the three Winter girls, Bessie, Bella and Mary, naturally, were packed off to boarding school in England. School was a lovely old country house that had been the home of Tennyson's friend, Arthur Hallam, for whom he wrote 'In Memoriam'. Holidays, very happy ones, were spent in Scotland with the families of school friends. The journey to England and back on the sailing ships of that time was long and arduous so holidays in Guiana were out of the question.

It must have been an unforgettable time for the sisters. Growing up in England. Long summers spent in Scottish country houses. Tennis parties, garden parties, riding. Boating on the lake. Cooling drinks on the terrace after tennis, the talk going on until the sun slipped behind the misty mountains and the dressing-for-dinner bell rang. There would certainly have been Balls, they were not too young to be excluded from Balls, and there would have been many of them. There would have been handsome, very handsome, attentive young Scotsmen in kilts. And, of course, they had the distinction, the quite unique distinction of being three young sisters who came from far-away Demerara 'where the sugar comes from.' The name of Sir James Spearman Winter would, of course, occasionally be heard in the conversation of the older people around them.

But schooldays came to an end and it was time for the three young ladies with their background of exclusive boarding-schools and holidays in Scottish country houses to return to that same Demerara. The mind can barely imagine the culture shock that must have been.

After weeks at sea—the filthy, crowded stelling. The swarms of dark-skinned people rushing ceaselessly around, shouting in a tongue so strange and foreign. The heat, the smells, the noise. Always the noise ... the whole unexpectedness of it all. The dusty carriage that awaited them when they were hustled through the crowds, the drive through a town they had almost forgotten. To the house by the sea, to Avalon, to their home. In Demerara.

The sisters were now considered equipped to take their place in the social life of the Colony and to marry qualifying sons of the elite. Alas, in their eyes no one was elite enough and no sons qualified. The Misses Winter felt themselves too good for those who wanted them and no one they thought good enough showed any interest in them.

So the three girls stayed at home in the big house by the Sea Wall and grew genteelly older, and were Old Man Winter's pride and joy. His wife was now dead and his sons embarked on diverse careers of their own, but his daughters remained for him to lavish gifts on—fine silks from India and China, laces from Europe, jewellery from the goldsmiths and silversmiths of England. He imported these treasures in threes, so if there was a silver locket inscribed 'Mary' you could be sure there was also one marked 'Bella' and another 'Bessie'.

The sisters took part in the social whirl which, in the Colonies, was never-ending. There were Balls and Receptions at Government House and at the military barracks where one could dance with the young officers, so very much like the young men one had met at the homes of school friends in Scotland … and **so** much more refined than the overseers from the sugar plantations. Oh, so much more refined! The Misses Winter never cared for overseers. If they showed the correct degree of poise and polish they were immediately labelled Remittance Men.

'Remittance Men—?'

The words had a romantic sound about them but Aunt Bessie quickly put us right.

'Shady characters.' A shudder. 'Undesirables. We do not speak of them.'

We learned from our parents that Remittance Men were characters of those times, exiled to the Colonies to atone for some dreadful sin in their mysterious past and to erase them from the memory of their families. Aunt Bessie spoke neither of nor to anyone she suspected of being one. There were, of course, a great many ordinary English, Scottish and Irish boys going out to the Colonies then, young men with a taste for adventure and a yearning to better their lot in life. But these were not the sort of people the Misses Winter wished to know.

Like the other ladies of the town, the Misses Winter drove out daily in their carriage. They left engraved visiting cards on silver salvers at homes of their choice and took afternoon tea if the lady of the house chose to be At Home. On Easter Monday and Whit Monday they went to the Races, clad in their very best silk dresses. On Sunday, dressed in their Church Dresses, they went to church. And in the early evenings when the sun was low in the sky but before it dipped below the horizon, they strolled on the Sea Wall, where they met and chatted with other ladies of colonial quality and the wives of the English and Irish officers of the regiment forming the Colony's garrison. Another opportunity for the sisters to show themselves a cut above the local ladies because they were not Creole, not having been born in the Colony, but coming from Abroad like the military wives.

The Sea Wall was the favourite gathering place at that time of day. Its initial purpose was to keep out the spring tides but it also made a very pleasant venue for a late afternoon stroll, especially when one lived in a malaria-hole like Georgetown. Then too, the children were always a joy to watch as they played on the sand in starched white dresses and sailor suits, supervised by their nannies, always navy-clad in their nannies' uniform and wearing wide Panama hats.

Mary died while still quite young. Then the quiet serenity of the sisters' lives came to an end with the death of their father. His sons had shown no interest in his import/export business and sugar prices fluctuated wildly on the world market, beet taking its toll of sugar cane. Winter and Company took down its shingle on Water Street.

The gold mining claim their eldest brother had staked in the interior appeared to run out of gold. The big house near the sea was sold. The sisters opened a school for the children of the wealthy, not far from their old home. For a dozen years or so they earned a certain measure of fame in the Colony for the quality of education they dispensed, the old-fashioned courtesies they taught and the high standard of discipline in their school. Then eventually they were too old and shortsighted and too hard-of-hearing for this also.They lived in a tiny rented house surrounded by remnants of past glories. We little girls tiptoed carefully in that tiny house, cautioned by our elders not to slip on the highly polished floor and break some irreplaceable treasure. Pieces of beautiful old furniture highly polished, the smell of beeswax heavy in the air. China vases, gleaming crystal, a little silver bell to tinkle when they wished the maid to serve afternoon tea. The tea service itself, with a tray so polished you could see yourself in it.… With their school closed, Great-Aunt Bessie took it upon herself to make up for any deficiencies in Kathleen's education. Lessons in Table Manners and How to Walk Correctly were given daily. How to place one's legs when Sitting (modestly). Stories and Essays were written for criticism. The mysteries of Cross-stitch were revealed. The days of sewing Samplers had long passed but not for Great-Aunt Bessie.

Then Bella died and the old lady retreated more and more into the past. The Great War had not touched her much in this distant corner of the Empire, but the bobbed hair and short skirts and the new slang she saw and heard around her did. They horrified her. Because she preferred not to see or hear them she seldom left her home. A lonely old lady who had outlived all her friends, she talked more and more about her childhood in Newfoundland—she always pronounced it New-FOUND(pause)land, and her schooldays in England. Those Scottish holidays in grand country houses … the people she had met, the estates they had lived on, the maids who had been assigned to the three Winter girls, the care that had ben taken of their clothes. Their almost-but-not-quite ball-gowns.…

Her early days in the Colony were recalled (they bore no semblance to the days in Scotland), so was her father's devotion to his three daughters and the lovely things he bought them. Some of those things were still there, behind lock and key in The Wardrobe.

Among them, we knew, would be The Opals. We had heard—or rather, overheard—of The Opals all our lives. They were whispered about by our elders, referred to when times were hard.

In colonial Guiana times were frequently hard.

'If only Aunt Bessie would do something about The Opals … what use are they to anyone, just lying there?'

'Fancy keeping them in The Wardrobe!'

'Something should be done—an old lady of that age could so easily be burgled. Lawlessness is rife nowadays, the Colony is no longer the place it was.'

'I suppose they do exist—? Or do you suppose it's just an old lady's ramblings—?'

'Aunt Bessie does not ramble.'

The Kitchen knew more about The Opals than anyone.

'Old Mr. Winter, he collect those jewels from all over. All over the world, I tell you! The places he go to get those Opals! And why? To present them to his daughters to wear at their weddings, that's why! How the poor man was to know nobody want to marry them? That they turn out old maids?'

'Was me, I would marry anybody just to get jewellery like that. Anybody. Fo' true he have them mek up in sets?'

'In sets? Is true-true! They make up in necklaces, bracelets, rings, earrings….'

A collective sigh. 'Those Opals must be really beautiful.'

'Beautiful? I tell you, nobody in Guiana ever see anything like them!'

This was true. No one in Guiana had ever seen the Opals.

'They must be worth a lot of money!'

'Money? More money than you and me could ever dream of!'

The inevitable silence fell as they contemplated that sum.

But there had been no weddings and The Opals had never been worn. It never occurred to anyone to doubt their existence, in spite of the fact that they had never been seen.

Kathleen turned the key in the lock and opened the door. A small squeak of 'Oh!' was all she could manage. She stood still, her hand to her mouth while two younger heads leaned forward….

The contents of The Wardrobe were in chaos. As though

the past had been hurriedly thrown into it and locked away out of sight. Open shelves at the top were stuffed with boxes— clothing, ornaments and old letters tied with ribbon tumbled out. The drawers below were just as full.

The days that followed were days of wonder and excitement for the young girls, sadness and nostalgia for the old lady. Nothing of very great value emerged. We unfolded garments with care, peered into boxes and bags, felt along the fingers of gloves, shook things out. We found no fabulous jewels made up in sets. Instead, it was the cherished fragments of a long life that we carried to the old lady's bedside. To us, it was treasure more valuable than The Opals.

Amid the piles of old lace and yellowed photographs in crumbling leather frames, there was an ebony dressing case lined with red satin and fitted with crystal scent bottles and trinket boxes, their silver tops green with age. There were fine lawn handkerchieves with deep borders of lace, high button boots and long white kid gloves, now a delicate shade of parchment. And button hooks … lots and lots of button hooks. They puzzled us at first because we did not have a clue what they were, but it turned out that they were as necessary to life in the old days as the can opener is today.

Small pieces of jewellery emerged. Anything of real value would have been sold years before. Was that what had happened to The Opals? The family grew more and more convinced of it. Aunt Bessie did not speak of them and we, the little ones, never asked. But her face alone showed how much the pieces that were left meant to her. Perhaps the mementoes of her youngest sister touched her most of all, the little sister who had died so long ago. She turned the silver locket inscribed 'Mary' over and over in her hands, her face softening as never before, her control crumbling before the surging tide of memory.

There was a little gold cross set with a tiny emerald, and three ivory crosses, beautifully carved. A cedar box filled with jet buttons and brooches, black and sparkling, more pieces of carved ivory. Glass paper weights inset with delicate floral designs. A collection of silver propelling pencils, their tops set with amethysts. Visiting card cases, one of onyx and two of mother-of-pearl. Wide bracelets and belts of silver and ivory. But no Opals.

Two lovely fans—one of sandalwood, its scent long since departed but its red ribbon still intact, the other of ivory, exquisitely carved. They had come from over the seas, from far, far away. They had dangled from elegant gloved wrists ... perhaps fluttered demurely in church, provocatively in ballrooms. They spoke of intrigue and romance and sad, dead hopes ... as sad and dead as the withered rose petals they had been packed among.

Poor lost youth, laid quietly to rest.

Vanished Opals, never to be worn.

Great-Aunt Bessie did not live very long after she unpacked The Wardrobe. The neat bundles she arranged on the big mahogany bed were divided between the three nieces who helped her unpack. We knew, even then, that none of us would forget that time. The heat of the day outside pressing into the shady room. The sound of the sea. The old, old lady among the pillows.

A hot, sultry Guianese day. The scent of frangipani drifted through the open window, cloyingly sweet, oppressive, filling the room and lingering between the folds of the huge canopied bed. The tiny figure sitting stiffly erect in her long white peignoir and lace cap, hated that scent ... the scent of the tropics, so far removed from the wild winds and crashing seas of her native Newfoundland.

Or of that other land....

Was it, one wonders—was it, perhaps, the Highland mountains and the heather that she longed for?

Remarkably, for such an intelligent woman, Aunt Bessie lived and died an exile, actively choosing to remain a foreigner, never taking her place with the sun and the strange exotic birds and the ever-blooming flowers of this new country. This sunlit, strange, exotic land.

There were, sadly, all over the Colonies of the British Empire, so many like Aunt Bessie.

Having unpacked The Wardrobe and distributed the relics of her past, she seemed to decide it was time for her to go. Perhaps it was just as well. She died in the 1930s before her world, the British Empire, began to fall apart.

She had taught so much, had had so much to teach. Good manners. Thoughtfulness of others. The gracious, graceful ways of living, all the things she had learned in her youth. She had not, sadly, learned what all colonials had to learn in order to be happy in a land far from home: to identify with that land, to learn its ways and love its people. To be proud of it. To like— to enjoy!—being there. To keep old memories, yes … but not to cling to them.

She died alone in that great canopied bed, the frangipani blossoms white and waxen in the moonlight outside her room. Perhaps, with death, her spirit soared through the open window, above the palms and flowers and soft breezes of the tropics, over the warm blue waters of the Caribbean … to the wild winds and waves and the rocky shores of another land.

Or maybe—maybe—to that place where she had spent the happy, long-remembered summers of her youth—that other land of purple heather and mist-clad mountains.

Chapter Four

A red dust road led into Enmore. It was long and straight and flanked by what looked, to a small child, like sheer drops into nothing. Land stretched away on either side, arid and brown and dotted with ant-hills, land where a lone goat might be tethered or a dispirited cow wander in search of sustenance. 'Pastures' we called them, those expanses of prickly, withered vegetation, and I never heard those biblical words about being made to lie down in green pastures without a feeling of alarm.

At the end of the red dust road a pair of enormous white gates stood. They were the entrance to the Compound where the staff houses lay and right behind them lurked the watchman in his white-painted shelter. There was always a long wait while he peered into the car and pretended he didn't know who the two children inside could be.

'Eh-eh! A boy from Queen's College? A l'il sister? But who dese children?'

Moments of pondering, head-scratching. The clanking of heavy chains as he undid the gates and finally a comic salute, standing stiffly to attention as we were driven through. (We had to reward him with uproarious laughter and energetic waves, in case he didn't let us through the next time.)

The overseers' bungalows lay on the left, quite separate from the managerial staff. They had bungalows by then shared by two or three overseers, the Quarters belonged to history. The Clubhouse and tennis courts were there also, and the Pay-office. This was the part of the Compound we looked at with interest, this was where things Happened and Life was Lived. On the right lay the houses that belonged to the management staff—more enormous white gates, lush, well-tended gardens, high hedges, palm trees brushing their fronds against the sky. In one of them The Kitchen waited on a Friday afternoon to welcome Master Bobby home on his return from Queen's College in Georgetown.

Indoors, the ice in the wide-necked Thermos would have melted—'that last piece is for your father's rum-and-soda this evening Miss Pam, **don't you dare touch it,** Rose's Lime Juice with boiled water for you.' The meat, delivered every morning from Georgetown, may well have been suspect, so dinner would be a tasty saltfish and onion cook-up, rice with greens, maybe a vegetable-and-potato curry, and perhaps cold baked custard with fruit to follow.

Dry provisions could be bought locally from the few shops on the plantation. Rice, English Potatoes (they were always called English Potatoes), salt, coffee and green tea, all could be bought in small quantities, even in twists of paper (known as 'twisses'). Larger orders were taken to Town by Bechu Lal, the estate messenger, and were delivered the next day on the morning train; there was also a regular daily order for ice and meat.

The railway in Guiana is the oldest on the whole South American continent. The first five miles cost £127,000 to build (in 1848!) which probably made it, at that time, the most expensive railway in the world as well. The biggest drawback to progress was that locals would not work for $1 an hour, so labour had to be brought in (at some cost) from the islands to complete it. Another problem that loomed almost as large was the absence of women. The firm in its generosity (or perhaps in its despair) threw up brothels along the route. These are said to have flourished, for trade was brisk. It is not surprising that the railway got so far and no farther. The money ran out spectacularly. The Project Engineer, Frederick Catherwood, went on to Central America where, with John Lloyd Stephens, an American, he embarked on a more ambitious project, ongoing to this day—the discovery and unearthing of the ancient cities of the Mayans.

The railway in Guiana was heavily used, both by passengers and for transporting sugar to the docks in Georgetown. Railway stations were busy, noisy, colourful places. They buzzed with East Indian women and children selling their goods to passengers: home-made curries wrapped in roti, dahl, cones of peppered channa, brightly-coloured coconut cakes, and best of all in that hot climate, **coconut water.** The top of the coconut was sliced off with a sharp cutlass and If you were fussy you got a straw, otherwise you just put the coconut to your mouth, put your head back and drank, praying that your mother would never hear of it.

(But she did. Years later I learned that she had always known about it: the plantation children on the East Coast were so few they were known to everyone. 'You never scolded us!' I said in wonder. My mother replied, 'Did you never notice that it was always the same woman who handed you the coconuts? That was Ramnarine's mother-in-law'.)

The newspapers and mail arrived daily by train, so did the order from the Demerara Meat Company. There was also a huge block of ice (from the Ice House) wrapped in sacking and sawdust. It had to be huge to allow for delays and meltdown on the journey. The estate dray-cart lumbered out to meet it in the early morning and lumbered back in the noon heat. The later it was, the more faces appeared looking out of kitchen windows. Some wag had named the dray Why Worry, scrawled in chalk on the sides. When at last the precious ice and meat was brought up the back steps to The Kitchen, it was swiftly seized upon and unwrapped to see how badly it had deteriorated during the journey. Loud cries if the meat was found to be 'off'—'Not fit for Puppy's food even, Mistress!' (All household dogs were known as Puppy by The Kitchen.) The ice had to be washed clean of sawdust (with boiled water, of course) while my mother worried about whether those people in the Ice House had actually boiled the water to make the ice. Then it was broken into chunks to be put into the wide-necked Thermos.

The ice-pick was kept on the wall on two high, safe hooks, in the manner of a trophy fish. It could not be easily reached. Even the grown-ups had to get on a stool to get it down. For the ice-pick was not just an ice-pick, it could be a lethal instrument, a deadly weapon. It figured in tales of murder and madness. I remember it as being long and pointed, over one foot long, and looking like an elongated, giant corkscrew with its sharp, shining point. A long, sharp, shining point, a deadly point. Chasing straying husbands or wives was just one of its alternative uses. I used to imagine it dripping with blood.

At party time a vast amount of ice had to be ordered for churning the ice-cream. Ice-cream churns were wooden tubs with an inner cylindrical container made of metal, with a tightly fitting lid and a handle at the side. Pieces of ice, heavily salted, packed the space between the tub and the cylinder, which was first cooled then filled with the ice-cream mixture, a luscious concoction of milk, eggs, sugar and The Kitchen's secret ingredients. That was only the beginning. Some lucky child, sometimes a group of children from the estate, keen to make a few pence, would take up a position under the house and sit turning the handle. Forever.

I remember the making of ice-cream as being a day-long procedure, but that can only have been my impatience to get at the end product. The churners were just as impatient and the cylinder was often opened surreptitiously to see how things were progressing inside. While it was opened there seemed to be no reason everyone should not dip a finger in and taste it. . . This caused mayhem in The Kitchen when it was discovered. Aprons flapped, voices were raised, feet ran back and forth, up and down the back steps and up again.... Fists were shaken, threats were made.

My mother thought that letting the churners have another ice-cream churn for tasting and payment would solve that problem but alas, there was no guarantee that The Ice House could deliver such a large order of ice. So the churners were made to sit where The Kitchen could keep an eye on them and give warning shrieks from time to time.

The Kitchen held a shifting population. Servants came and went, it seemed to be their way of life. The hardcore remained, but it was noticeable that the population shifted more rapidly when Aunt Vic arrived to stay. My mother always felt that had it not been for her sister the Servant Problem would not have existed, certainly not in our household. She dreamed of being served loyally throughout her days by grey-haired retainers, the way it always seemed to happen in books.

On her arrival at our house and even before the hat was off

her head, Aunt Vic would turn to look the current cook-in-residence up and down. Slowly. Once out of The Kitchen but always within earshot, she would demand of my mother just **who** that person thought she was.

'Now, Vic.' This occasion called for my mother's ready-to-wear Pained Look. 'Elvira/Edith/Hortensia has been doing very well since the last girl ... left. **You** remember. She ran out of the back door and down those long steps screaming—yes, screaming!—and saying that you ... well, never mind what you did or said. We want no trouble in The Kitchen, please, not this time. This girl is a good plain cook.'

'I see. **That's** what she calls herself. A cook.'

Then came the deciding question, the one that separated the women from the girls, the cooks from the call-themselves cooks.

'She can cook pepper-pot—?'

Pepper-pot is to Guiana what curry is to India. A traditional dish but more than that, a stew of meat and pork and what-have-you that can go on stewing for weeks, months, years. Centuries, even.

Cassareep is the magic ingredient which keeps it going. This potion is made from the juices of the bitter cassava tuber—poisonous juices. The juice is then boiled until it becomes syrupy, when it ceases to be poisonous and becomes casareep. Its magic is explained by the fact that the end product, the syrup, is a truly phenomenal preservative. It was the Aborigines who discovered that this deadly extract could be made edible (at what cost we do not know). Legend has it that there are caches of pepper-pot throughout the bush, which provide meals for hunters who then add their own bush-kill to the pot to keep it going.

In the days before refrigeration, in a country where travelling was difficult and communication more so—a country where those travellers turned up unexpectedly and often had good reason to stay for days—like waiting for a delayed government official, or an attack of malaria or the observation of deadly giant spiders—pepper-pot was the great standby dish. In some families they were said to be handed down from generation to generation and legends grew about their antiquity. At Diamond, one of the sugar plantations, there was a pepper-pot which was said to be **in its second century.** That one was carefully nurtured, exhibited, and tasted from time to time. The mind boggles to think how old the Aborigine pepper-pots must be.

Aunt Vic was a pepper-pot cook of some renown in our family. The stew was cooked in a large earthenware pot, used for pepper-pot and only pepper-pot, and dished out with a special long-handled spoon (also used only for pepper-pot) onto a bed of rice. There would be a side dish of greens if it was to be served at table as a meal, or it was often just eaten with bread as a snack. My brother snacked constantly on Aunt Vic's pepper-pot which pleased her; like all cooks she liked to see others enjoy her cooking. I couldn't stand the stuff, so confirming her belief that I was not a bright child.

My mother insisted that our pepper-pot should always be eaten fresh, and never kept for more than twenty-four hours, which gave rise to many a toss of the head and a suck-teeth from Aunt Vic, who liked the idea of her pepper-pot being passed down the centuries. The cook-in-residence, or The Girl as my aunt would insist on calling her, was not allowed to make pepper-pot.

The Girl, usually a stout, middle-aged person with no pretensions, would carry on cooking when Aunt Vic came, turning out steaming pots of rice, roasting cassavas and dishing up corned-beef rissoles and greens, unaware that she was in the presence of one of the great cooks of the world.

And she was. I, too, was unaware of it, foolishly supposing that the earth was peopled by others who could cook as my aunt cooked. That their curry—roti—dahl-puri and pepper-pot—their garlic pork, their cook-up rice—their souse, their mettemgee—all would be of the same long-remembered, longed-for taste.

They were not and never have been.

But hers was a cruel genius that mocked the commonplace in others. Poor Elvira/Edith/Hortensia at the stove was never able to answer Aunt Vic's scathing question 'Just **what** is that supposed to be?' A question which, when asked often enough of what was clearly a pot of rice or something equally basic, was sure to drive The Girl wailing from The Kitchen. 'What kinda question that is? Nobody ever ask me that before!'

Nor was I able to answer the still more puzzling question my aunt frequently put to me 'But, child, why are you so **Bad**?'

Aunt Vic believed in Badness. Most of the people she knew were Bad. They were snakes, vipers, or serpents; sometimes they were the devil himself. What was more, they had been born Bad, and no one believed in the concept of original sin more than she, not even the Roman Catholics themselves (Catholics were Bad). 'You're Bad!' she'd shriek at some luck-less child who had not had the time or opportunity to develop Badness. 'Yet,' she would add ominously when this was pointed out. '**Yet**.'

'Well. It's your look-out.' This, to my mother, on hearing that the person in The Kitchen was a new cook. 'Just as long as she knows my position in this household.'

Most people thought that Aunt Vic held the position of Unmarried Sister/Household Drudge. She worked very hard but never drudged and she was, in fact, married. She walked out on her husband a few days after the ceremony and began her nomadic life, helping Mrs. Su who made spectacular cakes for weddings and special events, sweeping into other people's kitchens and taking over, inhabiting the spare room until the inevitable heated exchange of words when she swept out again, straw hat roundly on head, cardboard suitcase in hand. 'All I possess!' she'd pronounce bitterly on arrival at our house.

'Not so,' my father would remind my mother, who'd be greatly upset by all this, 'All she possesses is scattered in sundry spare rooms around the Colony.' And God help anyone who laid a finger on any of those possessions, all neatly inventoried in her mind.

Aunt Vic had a son, Zack. Needless to say, he was Bad. I had every sympathy for him (I, too, was Bad) because I nev-er actually saw him do anything I felt to be seriously Bad. I have dredged my mind but come up with nothing, although I am told by those who are said to know that, yes, Zack was

Bad, Aunt Vic was not often right but she was right about that. When asked for details, I am given the answer only a Guianese can give—'Chile, if I tell you…' or 'Chile, **pray you never find out.**' I never did.

It would be satisfying to say that she was herself Bad. She was energetic, hardworking, and concerned about each and every member of her extended family, Bad as they all were. She was also highly entertaining which no doubt accounts for why her faults were always overlooked. Her quarrels lacked that eternal quality of Guianese quarrels, they never went as far as the grave and beyond; she cared deeply about the health of all those Bad people she knew and would drop everything to go and look after them if they were ill. Above all, she was a superb story-teller. You could be quite sure that twenty-four hours after departing with all she possessed, she'd be entertaining her new hosts with technicolour detail of the exodus, reducing them to tears of sympathy or helpless hysterics, whichever way the whim took her.

There were a few stayers in The Kitchen on whom Aunt Vic had no effect. Joseph was one, possibly because he was deaf and didn't choose to read her lips. He came at five o'clock every morning to light our stove. It was one of those cast-iron stoves that squatted bowlegged at the far end of colonial kitchens and roared at everyone; these stoves were famous for recognising no man and having no master. We were lucky that ours recognised Joseph. He alone could manage it. First, though, he had to chop the wood that it fed on so insatiably, and the steady thump-thump of his hatchet in the early morning was what woke the household. I lay waiting for the smell of woodsmoke to tell me that the stove was lit, that all was well and the day had begun. Then I went to sleep again.

Joseph brought the stove to life swiftly, effectively and with no lingering smell of kerosene. He was the only one who could do so, and The Kitchen was jealous of this.

'What has that Joseph's done to this stove!' Aunt Vic would shriek as it defied her from its rightful place at the end of the kitchen, roaring, rumbling and red-hot, daring her to go near it. 'The thing's going to EXPLODE! Look at it, it's red-hot! That man wants us all dead!' The Kitchen followed her lead, muttering about That Joseph when the stove cooled down and threatened to go out in spite of their kerosene-laden offerings. Joseph was frequently called from the factory where he had his day job as a labourer, to get it going again. On Sunday afternoons, when none of The Kitchen were about, he came in time to light it for our four o'clock tea and stayed to blanco and polish the shoes. He showed Bobby and me how to do so, and he also showed us how to get a brilliant shine on leather using banana skins or avocado flesh. This was useful during The War, when supplies of unnecessary items like shoe polish were scarce on sugar plantations although it was rumoured that they could always be found in Georgetown.

Sometimes Joseph remained to serve evening drinks. When the factory was not grinding (the term used when it was actually producing sugar) Joseph also served dinner. He put on a white coat with brass buttons to do so, although he never wore shoes. We loved the scuff-scuff sound made by his hard-soled feet. He liked us to call him the butler then, and we always did so. The Kitchen went along with it and it was amazing to see how swiftly a white coat with brass buttons could change their attitude.

Cookie was another stayer; she was the washerwoman. Once, indeed, she had been a cook, a very special one too. 'I went to Scotland with the Harpers,' she liked to remind people. They were the plantation chemist's family. 'I make dishes like Shepherd's Pie, Roast Beef and Yorkshire Pudding. Steamed suet puddings too and Creme Brulee. Properly. The way they should be done. None of your curry-and-rice, that's not what the English like to eat.'

But the Harpers had returned to Greenock, and there was no demand for Cookie's specialities in an 85-degree (Fahrenheit) climate. So she did our washing instead, turning up on Monday mornings beautifully dressed in old-fashioned servants' uniform. A starched grey dress that went down to her ankles. A wide white apron from which she always produced an envelope for me (her daughter Dulcie and I wrote back and forth, an earnest correspondence mainly about my dolls' health). When she took her hat off, it was replaced by a stiff white cap. This was the kind of garb other people's grand-mothers had once worn and long forgotten, and was now gaped at in amazement. 'Miz Wilsher, you go do washing in them clothes?'

She took over a part of Under-the-House with huge tubs, scrubbing boards, starch-pots and Reckitts blue-bags. Washing was a three-day event. It began with the making of lengthy lists of garments by my mother, who also had to hear complaints about their use. Cookie could always tell when the unforgiv-able sin had been committed—when something had been worn **more than once.**

'Madam, kindly look at this! What can Woman Billy be thinking of? The children's clothes—!'

'Imagine! We've all **worn our clothes**! What does that woman think clothes are for?' Aunt Vic's favourite question. On Cookie it had no effect, she simply went on washing, iron-ing, and laying down the law about the wearing of clothes (no garment **ever** to be worn more than once.) Clothes lines were scorned when it came to whites and bed-linens. These had to be spread out on the grass to be bleached by the sun and at her call The Kitchen dropped whatever they were doing to help with the spreading out. Panic struck when a curious cat or dog strayed over to have a look and a romp. The alarm would come from above— 'Miz Wilsher! Mind yo' washing!'

My mother worried about bete rouge, a little red insect that lived in the grass and itched fiercely when it got on the skin. She was convinced that it survived starching and ironing (so was I) but Cookie would do her whites and linens no other way. All that mattered was that they were spotless, stiffly starched, and put away in orderly piles in the linen press. 'And let the bete rouge bite where it may,' Aunt Vic would say with satisfaction, knowing well that the only person the bete rouge bit was me.

Wednesday was ironing day. The tubs and scrubbing boards were stacked away and the long pitch-pine table set up, covered with old blankets and something known as the 'ironing cloth'. A coal-pot with glowing red charcoal stood by to heat the heavy flat-irons. I seemed to be expected to burn myself to death on these as there was always concern about my whereabouts on ironing day. The smell of the hot iron on that freshly washed material was homely and comforting, and Cookie hummed or sang hymns as she ironed. She, too, counted her blessings ONE by ONE, or urged sailors to PULL for the shore, or else longed to meet others in the SWEET bye and bye.

The ironed clothes were laid on a large white tray and covered with muslin to be taken up the back steps, through the house and upstairs to my mother's bedroom, where they were laid on the bed and counted yet again. The washing and ironing done, the offerings made to the linen press, Cookie sat in the kitchen, her cap and apron off and her hat on, and became Christina to my mother and Aunt Vic, although I was never allowed to call her that. She was a tall, big-boned woman of Dutch descent, fair-skinned, with gentle grey eyes and great dignity.

She had tea and cake with us before she left, and told us yet again about her journey to Scotland with the Harpers. No one ever got tired of hearing about it. We heard about the ship, the long sea voyage and the weather gradually turning cold, and Cookie, who travelled Second Class, being allowed into the First Class section to look after Madam who had been seasick.

We heard about the glories of Scotland. The large Victorian houses with their rolling lawns. 'And the flowers, oh Madam, the flowers! Lilac, lupins, peonies....'

That was the part my mother liked best. That, and hearing about gardeners who **knew what they were doing**. My mother's own tropical garden was a brilliant sight, heady with fragrance, normally a delight to her, but on Wednesday evenings she could be found wandering among the bright blooms wearing a far-off look. Dreaming, no doubt, of lilac, lupins and peonies.

I went to Cookie's house once. Photographs had arrived from Scotland from the Harpers, and there was a large studio portrait of Jean. I was invited to have tea with Cookie and look at them.

The Kitchen was horrified.

'*Tea! With Miz Wilsher!*'

The invitation had The Kitchen abuzz. No one actually threw their aprons up and shrieked but they did the next best thing.

They **buzzed.**

Woman Billy was bombarded with comments, criticism, and advice on how to handle this unheard-of situation.

'But Billy … **is tek you tekkin the chile there?'**

'You actually tekkin the chile to the **range dwellings?** '

'How dis ting come about? Miz Wilsher invite the chile? Eh-eh! But what possess the woman! What 'bout all dis talk 'bout showin the chile only good tings? Dis ain no good ting!'

'Is bad—bad—BAD!'

'Put yo' foot down. Is time. If Miz Wilsher don't know better, and that surprise me I tell you, it really surprise me, then **you** do. **You** is the chile nanny, **you** is the one responsible.'

Woman Billy was in an unfortunate position, expected to carry out instructions by my mother yet expected to know better regarding those particular instructions by her peers. No small child, they felt, no child of the management staff, should ever set foot in the range dwellings. Woman Billy was given to hand-wringing when things became all too much. She wrung them now.

'Madam tell me to tek her. What else I going to do?'

'Fo' true, Madam tell you! But Madam ever been to the range dwellings? You tell me that!'

That, Woman Billy could not tell, nor can I. It is very likely that my mother lived a large part of her life at Enmore without ever setting foot in the range dwellings. Quite possibly she never even saw them. Many people did not. It was a time, a culture, when unpleasant things were neither seen nor spoken of.

The range dwellings were far out of sight of the road and the passing traffic, out of sight of the managerial staff houses and reached only by foot or bicycle. Woman Billy and I walked. Over the canal bridge where the punts brought the cane to the factory, through the village area where the rum-shop stood and the provisions shop with its Vimto and Radways Ready Relief sign, down the long straight path that led to the ranges, the canal on one side. Woman Billy wore a clean starched blue uniform, while I was carefully put into one of my better afternoon dresses and told not to get it crushed, which signified that this visit had importance, that Cookie was someone who mattered and was held in some esteem. Clean white socks, clean shoes, a big, shining new bow in my hair.

The range dwellers were not used to such sights.

Everybody was expecting us, there were waves and cheerful calls from some people. From others there were stilled bodies, silent looks and turned heads.

Cookie had a small house. They were all small, all of them joined up to each other, not houses at all, each really just a largish room. In Cookie's house curtains divided it into other rooms. There was lace at the windows, patchwork cushions on the chairs, a crocheted runner on the table where the recently-arrived picture of Jean Harper stood, Cookie's beloved Miss Jean. It was a black-and-white studio portrait, but I remember Jean as a gorgeous auburn-haired girl of whom Cookie was very proud.

There were other houses like Cookie's, lace-curtained, steps scrubbed. But only a few. All were black, unpainted. Some had brown paper pasted on the broken glass windows, torn sacking sagged from others. Some had no glass. Others had no steps. Most of them leaned crookedly because the stones that moored them had sunk unevenly into the ground. I clutched Woman Billy's hand all the time we were there, something I was not in the habit of doing.

The ranges were shocking. They had been built centuries before, to house the slaves. Rows of sour-smelling wooden dwellings stood on sour-smelling land where nothing grew. It is the smells I remember, most striking among them the smell of earth closets in that hot afternoon air. I had associated Cookie with the scent of soap-and-water and clean ironing, the imagined fragrance of lilac and peonies. So the smell of the ranges was more shocking to me than the sight.

Never could I have dreamed that places like those existed. Never. But they were there, they did exist, and they were actually **within walking distance of my own home.**

WHY?

Questions poured out of me when I got home. My parents seemed prepared for that, and quietly assured me I would understand it all when I was older—colonisation, slavery and its aftermath— but it was all too big a subject for me to grasp now. I was only a child.

I took my questions to The Kitchen who were plainly irritated by them.

'Look, chile, we busy! How you think we get food on the table? Where you think we find time to talk this nonsense! It all happen a long time ago, long before any of a'we born!'

Sometimes they said, 'Why you don' ask Annie-an-Susan these same questions you ask a'we?'

A'we' in The Kitchen were all the descendants of the African slaves, it seemed kitchen work was their speciality. Annie-an-Susan were Water Carriers, the girls who brought large containers of water to The Kitchen in dry weather. They also brought wide baskets of red logs which they delivered daily to the staff kitchens, these balanced miraculously on their heads. They were East Indian girls, young, long-haired, straight of back and beautiful to look at, and they made their deliveries swiftly and efficiently with no pause for chatter.

But I longed for conversation with girls of my age, not with Annie an-Susan. Not with the few visiting staff children from other plantations whose lives were so similar to mine, but with the children of the workers. How many brothers and sisters did they have? What did they do in school? What did they eat, did they really have curry-and-roti every day? We had curry only when my parents had informal lunch parties or, best of all, when the meat sent from The Meat Company in Georgetown had not survived the hot train journey and was 'off'. Then, we had only ground provisions to turn to and a curry sauce worked magic with these. It was especially magical with boring English Potatoes.

So I had no longed-for chats with the children on the plantation and I did not know how they lived. I had never seen a range-dwelling until that visit to Cookie and had known nothing about them. Cookie's place was laid out like a miniature house and she was the only person living in it at the time. I was amazed to learn that quite large families actually lived in one room, and not a particularly large room at that.

Sometimes, three generations might live in that one room and it was mainly this fact that ruled out any conversation with girls my age. Little girls who lived in one room with all their family knew and saw things they should not know and see. So I was told. Time and again I was told this, heads shaking.

So, of course, I had to know.

'What things?' I frequently asked.

'Things little girls like you should not know about,' Woman Billy told me sternly.

I grew aware of the oft-heard cry, 'When are THEY going to do something about those ranges?' 'THEY' being Booker McConnell, the owners of the sugar plantations. Later, when I was much older, I was told that the range dwellings were not the firm's responsibility. That, at any rate, was the argument put forward by the Company. Indentured labourers who arrived after the Abolition moved into the ranges the departing slaves had left or had new ranges thrown up for them. The freed slaves had not been evicted when their contracts ran out, they had been allowed to remain living in them if they wanted to. Rent-free.

Many of those freed slaves no longer worked on the plantations. They had jobs in Georgetown, in the Rupununi or in Brazil even—but their wives and families lived right there on the range dwellings while the bread-winners led lives elsewhere. Few could be bothered to maintain their homes on their return. They did not often return.

The plantation owners were still expected to look after the ranges but charity, they seemed to feel, stopped at free house maintenance. No, argued the range-dwellers, the plantations had built the houses which still belonged to them, on land which was still theirs, so it was their responsibility to maintain them. The argument went deeper. Centuries of slavery had developed a class of people entirely dependent on Them. So was it not all their fault—were They not doubly responsible?

I put the problem to a legal mind once. He thought about it and came back with his answer.

'I'll get back to you on that one.'

He never did.

Long after I left the Colony, I learned that a welfare fund had been set up to provide interest-free loans, and the ranges were being torn down and replaced by new modern houses. Now, I am told, the ranges no longer exist. A house by the water-side now seems to be a desirable place to live; some of the occupants have corials and paddle boats. I would not recognize the place.

So I am told. But I feel sure that if I walk over the canal bridge, past the rum-shop and the Vimto sign I would see them still. Long and low, close to the ground where nothing grows.

I can smell them still.

Chapter Five

Visitors were scarce. The English who came to Guiana to work on the sugar plantations would arrive in Georgetown not knowing a soul. If they were lucky they brought a letter or two of introduction to friends of friends. They then went directly to the plantation they were assigned to, met their half-a-dozen or so neighbours—and that was that. Until Christmas and Old Year's Night when the bigger plantations held large dances and the staff from the other estates were invited—and that was all. That was the sum total of social life, of mingling and meeting. The clubhouses and estate cars, billiard tables and bars came later. But in the Thirties there were only a few bridge fours and a great many early nights. Inter-estate travel, let alone socialising, was not encouraged.

The Company did not like it.

We were the only non-English family at Enmore and ours was an enviable position. We had relatives and friends we could visit in Georgetown and who made the journey out of town to visit us.

It was not a journey made on the spur of the moment and it was typical of the FitzGeralds, our cousins, that they undertook it so lightly, making impromptu visits when the mood seized them. It was an eighteen-mile drive on a road that was sometimes there and sometimes not, a road built of burnt earth that got washed away in the rainy season and blown away in the dry. Cars travelling on it broke down regularly and dramatically, always miles from the nearest village. There was seldom any passing traffic to hail for help. A distant cloud of dust could mean that another car or a donkey cart was approaching, or perhaps a straggle of hollow-ribbed cows, herded by a boy with a stick. We always travelled with a laden picnic hamper, bamboo fans and eau-de-cologne, well prepared for long, hot waits. Did the FitzGeralds have the foresight to do so too? Mummy doubted it.

It was on one of these visits that I discovered I was not an only child, which was how I thought my Aunt Marie referred to me, but a **lonely** child. At that age, I must have been six, only and lonely sounded much the same. It was Allan who explained it, amazed at my stupidity. (My brother Bobby had mysteriously become Allan on starting school and refused to answer to any other name. I learned that it was entirely my fault he had been Bobby at all, I seemed to have picked the name out of the air when I was barely able to speak.) He was nine by then, and devoted much energy to marvelling at my stupidity.

'How can you be an **only**? Only means one. See—one.' He held up a finger. 'There are two of us. Right? ' Another finger. 'So you're not an only. You're a **lonely**. See?'

I saw.

We were the only two staff children on the plantation and neither of us had playmates. Allan was being brought up like a man, and recently had been allowed to play with other boys on the plantation, all selected with discretion as these were workers' children, not staff. I was being brought up like a little lady and played with my dolls.

So the FitzGeralds' visits were landmarks in my life. My cousin Biddy was also Allan's age but she didn't play with him and Desmond, she was made to play with me instead. Reluctantly. The times the FitzGeralds came unexpectedly were the best of all. There were so **many** of them! They filled our house with chatter, laughter and stories of their life in Georgetown, a place I thought of as another world. There was Aunt Marie who was Daddy's sister and my beloved Uncle Johnny, Johnny Fitz my parents called him, the Irishman from County Clare who had travelled throughout South America only to return to Guiana to marry Marie. There was Pat, their eldest son, who had read every book that had ever been written and could explain about the stars and constellations, Terence who kept tropical birds and was later to be missing in the War. There was Mikey. There was Desmond, who was always urging others to be kind to me and not expect me to be as bright as they ('She's only little!') There were the girls, Kathleen, a vivid laughing head-turner, and Biddy who had no Woman Billy to say her yea or nay, just a nameless nanny (Nana) whom Biddy always seemed able to bully mercilessly. An enviable situation and I admired her for it.

Messages came on the single telephone line to the plantation and were relayed from the estate office to my father at the factory. 'Johnny Fitz and the family will be here on Sunday,' Daddy would tell us. 'Terence is going to drive.'

'Terence?' My mother's voice quivered. Her pink gin quivered. I knew the signs. She was about to say something disapproving.

She said it. **'Terence is going to drive?'**

My father nodded, he looked as though he wished he too could drive. But in British Guiana, in the thirties, one did not drive. Drivers drove. One was driven. That, at any rate, was how it was at Enmore and the surrounding plantations.

It seemed, though, that in Georgetown things were changing. Young men whose parents should have known better were getting behind the steering wheels of cars, driving around town in laughing groups, with girls. It was said that they went to the Sea Wall with supplies of beer and stayed there after dark.

That was not all. That was bad enough! But that was not all.

'We even heard, didn't we, that Kathleen was also learning to …' My mother's voice was hopeful, willing Daddy to remind her that it was just something we'd heard, this ridiculous rumour that Kathleen was actually learning to drive.

He took up his Edgar Wallace detective book instead and opened it at a new chapter. Daddy read aloud to us every night. Allan and I were not really expected to understand all that he read, although the stories were explained to us and there was emphasis on picking up new words and using them in context.

'Well,' my mother said, 'I just hope your sister Marie and Johnny Fitz know what they're doing.'

It seemed more important to us that Terence should know what he was doing, but we didn't say so. Children, one was reminded daily if not hourly, were meant to be Seen and not Heard.

'They won't like it in The Kitchen,' Mummy went on darkly. 'They haven't been given any time to prepare. You know how they love preparing. They like to take days doing it. I dread to think what Vic will say about this! '

'They will love it in The Kitchen. You know perfectly well there's nothing they enjoy more than a horde of visitors and a load of fuss, your sister most of all.'

'The Kitchen hasn't been given any time,' she protested, 'I tell you, James, I dread to think what Vic will have to say!'

It wasn't only those visited who looked forward to visits. The Kitchen would be throbbing with excitement. Confusion took over. Voices rose. Talk of food to be prepared and polishing to be done began days in advance. Would there be enough flowers for the vases? There was gloomy speculation as to whether the ingredients for the menus proposed would be available. I was kept far from The Kitchen when the actual cooking began. Tempers flew. Feet flew. People sang, sometimes they wailed. To deprive The Kitchen of this frenzy of activity was unthinkable.

'Nonsense, they'll love it. Your sister Victorene especially. Wait and see.' Daddy settled his glasses firmly on his nose. 'All that panic, all that rushing about. All those cakes that don't rise. All that time they haven't got! Now. Where were we?' And he would begin to read.

I loved the evenings. My parents and I sat at one end of the long gallery, Daddy in his Berbice chair (a 'planter's chair' in today's language) with a rum-and-soda beside him, Mummy in a bentwood rocker with a pink gin. Through the archway, Allan built amazing constructions with his Meccano set on the drawing-room carpet. In the blackness around us giant frogs croaked and night insects chirped, while the Delco, the generator that gave us electricity from 6 p.m. to 9 p.m., droned on and on.

I loved the sound of my father's voice as he read and the sound of words I didn't understand. I loved the smell of his rum-and-soda and the pink of my mother's pink gin. The moths fluttering in, the darkness outside … it was all magical.

I had no idea that in the eyes of my Aunt Marie and many other people, none of this was magical. Magical? Nonsense! In their eyes, I was a lonely child, one to be concerned about. A poor thing. No friends! No parties! No dancing classes!

But I did know how the conversation would go once the excitement caused by the arrival of all those relatives had died down, all those cakes and sandwiches and scones had been eaten, tea poured for the adults and jelly dished out for the young people, and Mummy and Aunt Marie sitting together. Everyone would be elsewhere but I had to remain with the two ladies for my aunt to see how much I had grown and what even more beautiful manners I had acquired since she last saw me. There was great emphasis on manners, no doubt some of it Aunt Bessie's influence.

'Have any families with girls of Pam's age moved onto the plantation?' Aunt Marie always asked. It was her first question and it seemed important. The answer was always no.

'So she still has no companions.'

There was little Eve at Cane Grove, my mother pointed out, she had been here with her nanny only a few months earlier and the two little girls had spent a nice time together. (The two little girls, in truth, had sat and looked dumbly at each other, neither being accustomed to company and not knowing what to do with it.) Then of course there was Jean Harper. She was much older, admittedly, and was at school in England but came home once a year. Or perhaps it was every other year....

At this point Aunt Marie would need a cup of strong tea and sometimes even strong drink. 'One of those pink gins you have yourself, Adrianna,' she'd say weakly. Aunt Marie was an early believer in mental stimulation for young children, in exposing them to the company of other children and to the cinema and the dancing class. My mother believed in ladylike accomplishments and quiet living. As we lived in a quiet place this was just as well.

Talk would turn to the Ursuline Convent in Georgetown, the school where Biddy went and Kathleen had gone and where, it seemed, I was also to go, although my mother had her doubts.

'But it's for Roman Catholics!' That was her biggest doubt.

'Where else is there to send her?' My father always asked.

There was no answer to that. There **was** nowhere else. The

Convent was the only boarding-school in the Colony and I came to realize that it wasn't a question of if I would go there, but when.

'In any case,' this was the point where my mother became defensive, 'James and I both feel that Miss Jackson will make a very good job of teaching Pam. Mr. Storey, the schoolmaster, highly recommends her.'

Miss Dorothea Jackson taught at Enmore school. Arrangements had long been made for her to teach me in the afternoons, but she had not yet started.

Aunt Marie, no doubt feeling it was time to change tactics, would look sympathetic and say she quite realized how hard it was for Mummy to let me go.

In those days, in a country that is now classed as Third World, babies were not always born alive. When they were, disease waited, ready to bear them off to churchyards full of tiny tombstones. My parents' first family, a boy and a girl, known to us as Sister May and Brother Jim, had died before Allan and I were born, Jim of an unidentified tropical disease, May of typhoid fever. Understandably, this had left my mother determined to keep me with her as long as she could although she accepted that Allan could not be kept at home (he being what was called locally a 'man child').

But her determination could not halt time. Allan was already cycling to the Golden Grove school many miles away, accompanied by a reliable man, Tegahli, who carried his lunch pannier. In due course he would go to Queen's College in town, perhaps travelling daily on the train, or maybe he would board in a carefully selected boarding-house and come home at weekends.

In the meantime, I was to be home-educated. A wooden screen was put up in the gallery, dividing it in half. We continued to sit in one half in the evenings, while a small table and two chairs appeared in the other half, then a blackboard and easel, then Miss Dorothea Jackson.

The Enmore school shut at 3:30 every afternoon, when Miss Jackson got on her sit-up-and-beg bicycle and rode over to our house to instruct me in reading and writing. I already knew how to read but I refused to learn arithmetic. There was no need, I explained to her carefully, Allan knew how to add-up and take-away. Quite how this brought me up to the standard of Form 1b at the Ursuline Convent I do not know.

Miss Jackson felt that her geography lessons should begin with the country we lived in. It was not possible for a six-year-old to take any interest in a place that was so small it couldn't even be found on the map. 'Look for the pink dot in South America,' she kept saying, adding proudly, 'The **only** pink dot.' She had to get out a magnifying glass to show me. Finally, I came to know that British Guiana was on the top of the right hand bump in South America between Venezuela and Dutch Guiana and that it was a very small place indeed compared to the rest of the world.

'Never mind how small we are,' Miss Jackson said, ' We have a unique address.' Our unique address was Plantation Enmore, East Coast, Demerara, British Guiana. Allan taught me to write The World, The Universe, after it.

Our postal system, too, was unique. The mail came from Georgetown on the morning train which left at 6 o'clock, stopped at all the villages and plantations on the East Coast, and reached Enmore, sixteen miles down the line, about five hours later. Letters went to the estate office and their presence there was broadcast by word of mouth.

'Madam!' Someone in the know would shriek at our back gate, 'You get a letter! A letter come! It there in the office!' It would later be delivered by hand, by the office manager, but by that time many people knew that Madam had got a letter.

'Dreadful.' My mother would protest, 'Quite dreadful. Having everyone know our business.' She stopped fretting only when reminded that not only were the envelopes sealed but few of the plantation population knew how to read.

Perhaps that was why they were all so passionately determined that their children should learn, not only to read but to learn every single thing there was to be learned. Perhaps that was why the Enmore school was too small from the first day it opened. Schoolmasters and teachers neither spared the rod nor spoiled the child, although their pupils' parents were convinced that they did. Those parents turned up at the school regularly to plead with Authority to beat their children—'To mek sure he **learn**, Schoolmaster.' It was felt to be the only way.

Just in case Schoolmaster wasn't up to it, the children were given an extra dose of beating ('licks') at home. The parents' authority was biblical. Their wrath was biblical. Their language was biblical. They didn't beat their children, they didn't even give them 'licks'—

They CHASTISED them.

They could be heard chastising them every day of the week. When the stillness was suddenly pierced by the sound of shrieks, you knew that some luckless child was being held by the hair and swished about the legs with a Pointer, its feet hitting the ground so fast its legs were a blur. The quarrel was always the same—'Chile! Is why you don't **learn**! Is stupid you stupid?'

'Don't beat me, Ma, I beg you! Is beg I beggin' you, Ma, don't beat me!'

'I beat you till you learn! Y'hear—I beat you till you **learn**!'

There were two instruments of CHASTISEMENT. One was the Pointer, the thin, flexible spine of the coconut frond. When stripped of the leafy bit, pointers were bound together to make brooms of all sizes which were found everywhere, at the bottom of the outside back steps, in the chicken coop, in the garden and in the kitchen.… There was no escape from anything that was so easily to hand. Applied to the legs, a single Pointer stung like a horde of red ants.

The Tamarind Rod was the other instrument, specially selected from young branches of the tamarind tree, honed with care and frequently tested through the air for swishability. It made an awesome sound. Pointers stung but the Tamarind Rod—**that** was something else. It was said to be the next best thing to the Cat o' Nine Tails.

'He get the Tamrin'' was reported in hushed tones among the children and everyone became solemn.

I never became hardened to the lot of the plantation children, although they themselves clearly did. Many of them were younger than I, and my imagination saw myself in their place.

I was at the age when I was convinced that Daddy could do and fix everything and pleaded with him to do something about those beatings.

The screams were dreadful.

'Those parents love their children, that's why they beat them,' he started to explain to me.

I was baffled. It made no sense. They loved them—? My bafflement expressed itself in a forbidden word, one that always froze everyone in their tracks when they heard me utter it, a word that caused my mother much pain, or so I was told repeatedly.

'Eh?'

He overlooked it. 'Because they love their children they are determined that they will never work in fields or in factories as they, the parents, do. They have nothing to leave them when they die, no house, no money, no land, nothing. Nothing. The only thing those parents can leave their children is an education. That is the only way for them to get better jobs and have better lives, through **education**. If they are educated then they will have a choice of what they do and where they work. The more educated they are the wider the choice. Nobody wants to employ dunces!'

A stern look here, a significant pause.

'One thing is quite certain—they won't have to work bare-footed in fields as their parents do, they won't have to live in range dwellings. They will have houses like we have, perhaps bigger and better.'

Another pause then: was I grasping it?

'Do you understand? Their parents are trying to give them a future, a better life than they, the parents, have. The children are too young to realise the importance of education—as you seem to be.'

Pause.

'That's why the parents try to beat it into them, they don't know any other way! Talking doesn't work, believe me. Don't worry, I won't beat it into you! But their way will work, you'll see. Many of those children will grow up to be dentists or doctors or lawyers, or businessmen in town. Those who don't learn

… well, they will have to work in the fields, ragged and bare-footed, just like their parents. And they will wish for the rest of their lives—the rest of the lives, I tell you, that they had learned when they were taught!'

He always finished by looking at me sternly over his glasses. I just hoped he meant what he said about not beating me.

I'd never thought of being anything but what I was, a small child at Enmore, loved and looked after by everyone I knew. It was a surprise to realise that things weren't always going to be so. That I was expected to be educated. To do and become something or someone.

'What shall I be?' I worried endlessly, but there was no problem finding the answer to that.

Under-the-House, they had it ready for me. It seemed, because I didn't learn my lessons, meaning my two-times tables, I was destined to be a Yard Granny. They were all convinced of it.

Yard Grannies are not to be confused with real Grannies, although this is easily done. In an attempt to avoid confusion, real Grannies were sometimes called by their surnames, that is Granny Adams, Granny Billings, Granny Carey. This led to more confusion, as nursery nannies, those very superior persons dressed in Panama hats and navy uniforms who wheeled their charges to the Sea Wall or the Botanical Gardens in the afternoons, were also called called by the family names, Nanny Adams, Nanny Billings, and so on. The words 'Granny' and 'Nanny' of course got mixed up, it was easily done. And as I mentioned earlier, in my mother's family, my grandmother was known as Mother to her children and also to her grandchildren, something which has caused confusion to this day.

Yard Grannies were the pensioners of the East Indian workforce. That is not to say they drew a pension after years of quite literally backbreaking work in the fields. It simply meant that it was recognized that after all those years working they had the privilege of **going on working** in order to live. So they were given more work.

All the staff homes on the plantations had a Yard Granny. They turned up at dawn to clean out the chicken coop (at dawn, just in case you thought they weren't coming and gave the job to someone else), to sweep the front and back steps, and supposedly to spend the rest of the day cleaning the chicken coop and whisking the gravel about with a pointer broom. (Interestingly, our 'gravel' on the plantation was made of crushed sea shells.) In reality, they vanished to a cool corner of the garden where they dozed and dreamed, only to appear when there was a call from The Kitchen—'Granny! Here's your breakfast!' Or lunch, or tea. Huge slices of bread, spread with margarine and marmalade (our Yard Granny preferred imported English marmalade to the kind The Kitchen made). Great steaming tinnin mugs of coffee, smelling as coffee has never smelled to me since.

Now, when I rake the gravel on the driveway, I remember being threatened with Yard Granny status. I remember that call to breakfast. To coffee and to warm home-made bread with real English marmalade.

How I wish I could hear it.

Chapter Six

From time to time, Teacher Milly came to visit. She had taught at the nearby Golden Grove school where her father was headmaster and my mother had been one of her pupils. Like Georgetown, Golden Grove was one of the outer limits of my world. An exciting place with wide dusty roads where cars swirled and screeched, colourful Indian bazaars, noisy rum-shops, delicious smelling street-food and shave-ice stalls. Excitingly, unbelievably, it also had a cinema.

Now on her own, Teacher Milly was a spinster, thin, straight-backed, straight-faced, straight-laced. Long sleeves buttoned at the wrist. High collars buttoned at the neck. Teacher Milly also ate **very slowly.** Each mouthful was chewed fifty times; she informed us that this was called 'masticating'. Once the fascination of counting her chews wore off meals became tedious. They also became lengthy, four o'clock tea threatening to merge with children's early dinner. My father always had a legitimate excuse to leave the table as soon as he'd eaten for Teacher Milly always came when the factory was at its busiest. No doubt the timing of her visit was neatly arranged so it did not seem out of the ordinary that he should leave the table with words of false regret and a flourish of best napkin. There was always the best of everything when Teacher Milly visited.

There was an air of assessment about these visits, as though the teacher was summing up her pupil, checking progress and seeing whether standards were being maintained. We were expected to be on our best behaviour and not do anything to let Mummy down.

Teacher Milly had known our Sister May and written in her autograph book. I used to ponder the words in handwriting as upright as Teacher Milly herself. They meant nothing to me then, although the grownups laughed at my mystification and assured me that they would, oh undoubtedly, one day they would!

And one day, quite suddenly, they did. Ominous, haunting words, their meaning grows clearer by the day.

My mother's teacher wrote—

'You shall do so much in the years to come,
But what have you done today?'

It was Teacher Milly who told us about the Masquerade Bands. She visited a different Georgetown to the one we knew and she saw places and sights we never saw. Her accounts of the Masquerade Bands were vivid, her words excited me as nothing else she told us did. Each time she told us I actually saw the bands and the dancers in even gaudier colours than I'd seen them before—I heard the music—heard the drums—louder—louder—louder.

The dancers were all men. They were brilliantly dressed with high blonde wigs, and made up as women. Pale painted faces, mouths a bright scarlet streak, glittering jewellery made of shells painted silver and gold. They pranced the streets of the Georgetown I did not know, they danced on high wooden stilts wearing enormous hooped dresses, giantesses in dazzling costumes of long ago. The band wore coats of scarlet and gold and green, and bright white papier-mache faces, they drummed and whistled and played strange instruments that real orchestras had never heard of.

The crowds followed their drumming, growing larger by the minute, some people just running and laughing behind and beside them, but most of them dancing too until the whole street, as far as you could see, was a swirling, whirling line of dancers, the street thudding under their feet like a dance floor, the dust rising thickly among them. There was music!—music!—and laughter everywhere! Oh, the beating of the drums! The flashing, dazzling colours! The laughter! The music and laughter and the drums!

So Teacher Milly said. It sounded fantastic.

I longed to see it.

I knew it was unlikely that I ever would. People dressing like that—behaving like that—**excitement like that!**—could only be imagined. It did not exist in my tiny world. I could only dream about it.

One day it was rumoured that a Masquerade Band was on its way down the coast from Georgetown. Mr. Motoo, the pedlar, was the first with the news. I had to keep indoors if they came, I was warned in The Kitchen, because it was well known that the dancers whirled little children up under their enormous skirts, whirled them away and *they were never seen again.* Perhaps it would be better if I hid myself and didn't let them see me—and I didn't see them!—just in case they came back after dark.…

I didn't care what warnings they gave—the Masquerade Band was coming to Enmore!

I was going to see them at last!

The gaudy giantesses! The bull-headed man who roared and charged!

The drummers in scarlet!

The laughing, dancing, hollering crowds!

They would fill the roads! They would dance in the sunlight! Everyone on the plantation would join them, the whole place would be a whirlwind of colour and drumming and—!

Oh, the thrill of it! The anticipation!

They came in the still of noon, along the dusty quiet road.

We heard the thin fluting, the far-off drumming, saw the approaching blob of colour that flickered and shimmered in the heat. It was a very small blob.

They took a long time to become distinct. As they came closer we made out a trousered man who carried his skirts thrown over one shoulder, his stilts over the other. The bull-headed man in his tattered costume. (The bull's head was carried on the man's back, like a rucksack, the horns pointing outward.) A solitary drummer, a man with a flute.

A single dancing boy.

We watched in silence from The Kitchen. In the back yard, where they had been allowed because we children were so keen to see them, the five masqueraders performed, a small faded group. The giantess pirouetted in shabby skirt and wig, the bull roared tiredly. The dancing boy leapt and spun without enthusiasm. I looked on from behind the grownups' skirts, half-afraid that if they saw me they really would come back in the dark to whirl me away. But—

The bedraggled band had a magic and a menace I still do not understand. The drums, perhaps? Old people in the country always crossed themselves at the sound of far-off drumming. In olden days, the days of slavery when Africans escaped into the unknown regions beyond the populated fringe, their presence in that darkness was known only by the beat of drums. Some ancient knowledge stirred at the drumbeat—perhaps the genes remembered. People felt silent. Eyes rolled, the sign of the cross was made.

The masqueraders were given cold drinks of lemonade Under-the-House and coins were dropped into their rattling tin. The giantess took off his wig and skirt and slung his stilts over his shoulder. Then the band straggled away.

There was silence in The Kitchen as everyone went back to what they had been doing.

'Eh-eh!' A long suck-teeth.

That was all.

Various members of the band had dropped off to visit relatives along the way, we heard later. What we had seen was just the straggling residue, the people who had no relatives on the coast to visit but came this far in the hope of collecting a few coppers. I was not to be disappointed, they told me Under-the-House, so clearly disappointed themselves. Perhaps Miss Milly had painted it bigger than it was, they said, or perhaps she was remembering how the Masquerade Bands had been a long time ago when she first saw them. The Lord knew it was years and years since Miss Milly was a girl and first saw them. Things changed. Perhaps we had all expected too much.

What **had** we expected?

Later, lifetimes later, under a black Brazilian sky—black, because the stars vanished before the brilliance of that Cuidade Maravillosa, the Marvellous City— I watched the breathtaking marvel that is Carnival in Rio. The crowds, many of whom had seen it all before, indeed saw it every year, gasped collectively at the sight of every new float that went by. The Bahian ladies on their stilts swirling their huge white skirts—the exotic plumed dancers who glittered and pranced—the others who leaped and spun—the brilliantly costumed women—such beautiful women!—and men stomping and swaying non-stop to the beat of drums … scenes of glitter and colour and movement that made those seasoned crowds gasp and cheer and roar.

Under that Brazilian sky I saw again the sad little Masquerade Band of that long-ago day at Enmore, exactly as I had expected to see it. Exactly as I had pictured it in my mind. Perhaps that was how the masqueraders, the giantesses and the drummers in scarlet, the leaping boy, had pictured themselves too.

Teacher Milly had a long-lasting problem with mangoes. After her parents died she lived alone in the house. She could not always make ends meet and could not afford to get someone in to clean the yard. In the mango season the fruit fell steadily from the trees, the ground grew thick and yellow and even the thieving boys who vaulted the fence to run off with their loot could not clean up the mess.

It was impossible to sell the fruit or even give the mangoes away. In a good season the mango trees everywhere in Guiana bore profusely and kept on bearing. The rotting fruit gave off a sweet, sickly smell, a pervasive smell that hung about in that hot air that never moved.

Neighbours complained.

'Miss Milly! Yo' yard SMELL!'

Advice on dealing with the problem ranged from cutting the trees down to getting a lodger who could be made to keep the yard clean as part of his rent. Such a lodger did not appear. There seemed no answer. But on one of her visits we heard that the perfect solution had been found. An old woman from a distant plantation, one long derelict, was going to make the journey to Golden Grove to talk to Teacher Milly's mango trees.

'To talk to the trees—?'

Even Aunt Vic had never heard of this. In The Kitchen, they drew great breaths then let them out in hoots. They clutched each other and clutched themselves, they tottered down the back steps, still hooting.

The old woman would explain the situation to the trees, Teacher Milly told us, and ask them to refrain from bearing fruit while she, Milly, lived there. The trees would continue to grow as green as ever but **would not bear mangoes again.** It was as simple as that. Nothing to do with obeah or black magic, she assured us, as faces darkened around her and significant glances were exchanged. The old woman was simply someone who was in tune with Nature and whom Nature obliged from time to time.

'Poor Milly,' I heard Mummy say to Aunt Vic, 'She really is getting old. Pray God we don't become like that.'

For once, Aunt Vic was speechless. She just shook her head.

On one of my weekends home from boarding school, I remembered the laughable tale and asked about Teacher Milly's mangoes. They were no longer a problem, I was told, the trees had stopped fruiting ages ago. Hadn't I heard? A country-wise old woman, one of those rare people in tune with Nature, had asked them to stop.

I laughed and laughed, hearing again the howls and hoots of The Kitchen running down the back steps, remembering Aunt Vic's face.

My mother looked at me sternly. 'No need for that,' she said, 'There are a lot of things in this world we don't understand. The Old-People know some things we don't.'

Mr. Motoo, the pedlar, plied his dusty East Coast route on a bicycle. He rode slowly from one village to the next, bent forward over the handlebars, his legs moving laboriously, his huge cardboard suitcases lashed on to the carrier behind him. He and his brother had a one-room shop in one of the remote East Coast villages and were said to have lots of money. Teacher Milly knew the family; it was Mr. Motoo who told her about the old woman who spoke to the mango trees. Mr. Motoo only took to the road on his bicycle to get away from his village, he often said. He would arrive in the early afternoon and after a long drink of iced water, open his cardboard case and festoon the ping pong table in our play area with exotic silks, strongly scented liquids in coloured glass bottles, little Chinese paper parasols, and tiny pink celluloid dolls with moveable limbs that were attached to the body with elastic thread. He had perfected the amazing trick of reaching inside his never-emptied case and producing whatever was mentioned.

If he so disliked his village, they asked him Under-the-House, why didn't he and his brother set up shop in Golden Grove, a thriving place with plenty of passing trade? They lived in that village because they had always lived there, he would explain, and so had his parents, now dead. That was good enough reason. It was where they slept, opened up, closed up and counted up. He did allow that sleeping, eating and counting their money in one room behind the shop as he and his brother did, meant that they got pushed for space.

'It's all those white shirts,' Teacher Milly said, 'No room for the Motoo brothers and all those white shirts.'

According to rumour Mr. Motoo and his brother wore only white shirts and changed them several times a day. A washerwoman pummelled daily in a tub behind the shop with Gossages soap and a scrubbing board, and there was always a line of washing, mainly white shirts, flapping in the wind. He and his brother also rode the latest model of the most expensive bicycles and a small boy was always on hand to keep them polished. There was talk of building a house with a laundry room underneath and a shed for the bicycles but it never got beyond talk; they were concerned, Mr. Motoo said, about the noise the builders would make, they were sure it would wake the Sleeping Woman.

We heard about Mr. Motoo's neighbour every time he turned up in the yard on his splendid bicycle to open up the magic bottomless cases. The Motoos were reluctant to do anything that might disturb their neighbour. If disturbed, heaven knew what a Commotion there would be. (Commotion: a popular word in the local vocabulary).

The Sleeping Woman was spoken of with grave faces and shaking heads and everyone wondered how anyone could sleep for so long. Sometimes, Mr. Motoo said, she came out of her room and sat on the verandah. Sometimes she rocked and sometimes she just sat still, but always the alligator sat at her feet. 'A sausage-dog, you mean, Mr. Motoo,' Woman Billy would say quickly for my benefit, 'One of those long dogs like a tube. Short little legs. Busy-busy. Yes, that's what it must be.' Mr. Motoo and those assembled said nothing. Over my head they just looked at each other and smiled.

Under-the-House, they knew all about it. The alligator, story had it, had come out of the trench that ran through the village and channelled water away in rainstorms. All sorts of things lurked in that water and in the high grass on its banks—giant rodents called yewarris, strange fish and, of course, alligators of all sizes. The alligator had come out one night and found its way onto the verandah, through an open space and into the Sleeping Woman's bed. In the morning they were found together. The maid who took her tea in ran screaming from the house and told the story everywhere, she swore the sight had turned her hair white in an instant. Nobody doubted it.

The bungalow where the woman slept could be seen from the road, through tangled hibiscus hedges and a garden gone wild. Some evenings the woman and the alligator could be seen on the verandah, she sitting in her rocking chair, the creature beside her, both of them quietly enjoying the breeze stirred up by the spidery fronds of the coconut palms.

It was one of those situations people said darkly they didn't like the sound of but enjoyed hearing about all the same. The account for the groceries was sent to an address on a coastal plantation and was paid promptly. There was no excuse for either of the Motoo brothers to go rapping on the door and perhaps unravel a bit of the mystery or maybe add to it.

'It was the children,' I'd hear. 'She took it bad when she lost them.'

I assumed her children had all died of some dread tropic illness, but we heard later, in one of Mr. Motoo's instalments of the story, that they had been sent to school in England. Suddenly, all together. She had stayed behind to be with her husband, like any dutiful colonial wife, but one day she'd found him with another woman....

She'd gone mad.

Another story had it that she was a local girl who married an Englishman on one of the sugar plantations. He thought she was pure-blooded English herself, she being blue-eyed and fair-haired, and she let him go on thinking so. But when the children were born there was evidence that she was far from pure-blooded English and he swore he would pay her back for the deception. Years passed. Nothing happened. They seemed a happy couple with a large, happy family.

One day when she was away visiting friends, all the children were put on a ship for England. They went straight into boarding-schools to be made into real English people and they were never coming back.

There had been none of the farewell rituals that colonial families went through when children left for school in England. None of those weeks with dressmakers and tailors getting clothes ready, old retainers coming to wish them a safe journey and be given cake and lemonade. She had not said goodbye to them. She didn't know where they were and she never would, he vowed.

An unhappy tale, but only one of the many Mr. Motoo brought. The worst was the one about a woman being found on the back-dam with her lover. Colonial ladies, pure-blooded English or not, never went on the back-dam, with or without their lovers. Even I knew that, even then. Perhaps that was what made it doubly awful, her being on the back-dam. At any rate, so Mr. Motoo's story went, her husband followed and pumped the lover full of gun-shot. He fell into the canal and was torn to pieces by the alligators, churning up the muddy red froth and lashing it about with their tails while she screamed on the bank and her husband laughed.

She collapsed into bed when he got her home, waking only briefly at times, times when the nightmare she woke to was so horrible she quickly fell asleep again. After some years and many visits to doctors abroad, her husband found the bungalow in the remote village where she was sent with her old Nanny. Men with cutlasses and rakes turned up occasionally to tidy the derelict garden, but it quickly became overgrown again. Once, the bungalow was painted.

Why, I wondered, had she taken an alligator to her bosom, quite literally, when its kind had eaten her lover? Did she think, perhaps, it was her lover come back in alligator form? I wondered this aloud to my mother. (I was older by then and could use words like 'lover').

'It's just one of that pedlar's more outlandish tales,' Mummy said dismissively. She was busy at her sewing-machine. Then she added, 'You don't want to believe everything you hear. You **certainly** don't want to believe anything you hear from Mr. Motoo.' The pedlar told these ongoing tales all the time, all the pedlars did, and for all she knew, they all told the same stories. As for the Sleeping Woman—!

She was simply a poor unfortunate, born to one of the English plantation families farther up the coast. Never been right in the head. She lived quietly in the small bungalow with her little dachshund, and the family's old nanny took care of her, as she was now getting older and more disruptive. Couldn't stand noise, apparently, noise sent her into frenzied fits of screaming. That was all there was to it.

This was terrible. It was as bad as hearing that there was no Father Christmas. I would rather not have been told.

There was a hilarious story we heard again and again, about the people who put out food at night for the Fair Maids. These were water spirits who numbered many in that land of many waters. I imagined them to be freshwater mermaids, more striking by far than the deep sea models. They were smaller and slimmer, as they had to fit into our creeks and trenches. Their scales were silver and their hair was silver too. They appeared under the midnight moon to shimmer and sparkle and change our muddy rivers and trenches into waterways of shining beauty.

You were lucky if you saw this sight, few indeed had ever

seen it. And if the Fair Maids asked you to do them a favour, then you were lucky indeed. For the Fair Maids could do terrible things if you didn't do as they wished, things like providing a watery grave for all the members of your family. That was just for starters.

The people Mr. Motoo told us about had only just moved into a small country village and were actually contacted by the Fair Maids shortly after they had put out the usual offering of bread and water by the creek. The spirits spoke to them from afar to say how much the offering pleased them and asked for a more lavish spread the next evening. Mutton curry was on the menu. They even specified that there should be a large amount of hot pepper. Bottles of beer were also requested. The offering was to be placed in the centre of a wide circle of candles where it would all be consumed by the Fair Maids. The providers did not need to be told to keep their distance. All manner of favours were promised if this wish was granted, the supplicants had only to ask.

The women of the household cooked all day to provide a sumptuous feast. The offerings were laid out in the circle as instructed, the candles lit and in time the Fair Maids appeared, ghostly white-clad shapes, wavering and indistinct in the flickering candlelight. They seemed to stumble and trip over their white robes as they had, of course, no feet. They had very good appetites though, for there was nothing left of the feast the next morning.

The family were mystified to find that the Fair Maids had left empty bottles of rum behind as well as a number of cigarette ends, and to find themselves greeted with jeers and laughter by the rest of the village. They were even more mystified when, in spite of repeated requests, the Fair Maids did nothing for them in return.

Above: Cutting sugar cane.
(Government of British Guiana
photograph, c. 1897.)

Right: "Sugar cane travels on punts
from the fields along the coastal
strip of Guiana to the factories
where it is processed. Sugar and its
byproducts—rum and molasses—
are the country's most important
exports. British Guiana ios unique
in harvesting two sugar cane crops
each year." (Photo and caption from
British Guiana Today [London: Her
Majesty's Stationery Office, 1956].)

Left: Plantation
Enmore, East Coast
Demerara, British
Guiana, c. 1900.
(Photo: H.K.L. von
Ziegesar, Georgetown,
British Guiana.)

Left: The author's parents, Adrianna and James Winter, the author, and her brother Allan. (Photo from the author's personal collection.)

Right: The author, her father, and her brother Allan.
Below: Enmore main house. (Both photos from the author's personal collection.)

Above: The Enmore sugar factory as seen from the east kitchen windows of the main house.

Below: Lama, headquarters of the East Demerara Water Conservancy, which was managed by the author's uncle, John FitzGerald. The roof was painted red and white shortly before World War II to offer pilots heading toward the U.S. base at Atkinson Field a landmark if they were off course.

(Both photographs from the author's personal collection.)

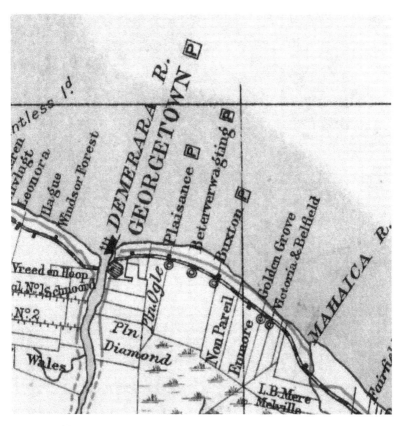

MAP OF
BRITISH GUIANA
PUBLISHED BY AUTHORITY OF HIS EXCELLENCY THE GOVERNOR
SIR GRAEME THOMSON, K.C.B.
Revised and corrected to date from the records of the
Department of Lands and Mines, Georgetown, Demerara
UNDER THE DIRECTION OF
HON. G. D. BAYLEY
Commissioner of Lands & Mines
1924

The location of Enmore (just to the right of Non Pareil and below Golden Grove) can be clearly seen in this detail from a 1924 map of British Guiana published by Stanford's Geographical Establishment, London, under the direction of the colony's Commissioner of Lands and Mines, George D. Bayley. The map's title card is reproduced below. (Original of map held in the University of Toronto digital map collection.)

Above: Author and cousin
Biddy FitzGerald on Lama
Creek, Lama.
Right: Cousin Biddy FitzGerald
"dressed for dinner" at Lama.
(Photographs from the author's
personal collection.)

Below: The author's ancestors at an 1882 Bel Air tennis party: Marion
Stokes, fourth from right in a white dress and small white hat; Rashleigh
Porter, immediately behind her; and Harry Stokes, to the left of Rash-
leigh Porter, in a grey hat with only his head showing.
(Photographs from the author's personal collection.)

Top: Main Street, Georgetown; Sacred Heart Church at far left.
Centre: Sea wall, Georgetown, originally built by the Dutch.
Bottom: Atkinson Field—the airport as we remember it.
(Photographs from the author's personal collection.)

Top: A Berbice chair.
Centre: St. Rose's Ursuline Convent, Georgetown.
Bottom: The Centennial Pageant at the Convent, 1948. A series of skits
starting with the founding of St. Rose's in 1848 and continuing with
significant events in its history.
(Photographs from the author's personal collection.)

Three Georgetown landmarks …
Top: The Girl Guide Pavillion.
Centre: The Rialto Cinema.
Bottom: Booker's Drug Store (on the left) and the
building housing *The Daily Chronicle* newspaper.
(Photographs from the author's personal
collection.)

Above: The author's father,
James Winter, c. 1930.
Right: A cane field.
Below: Workers, a mule, and
punts.
(Photographs from the author's
personal collection.)

Chapter Seven

Miss Dorothea Jackson taught me that Columbus discovered America. From Miss Florence McKinnon I learned that Sir Walter Raleigh had discovered Guiana. Raleigh had sailed from Trinidad down the Orinoco River and found a land ore-rich and mineral-rich—a land so rich in gold that its people were powdered in gold dust and its distant mountains glittered.

And it was called the Land of El Dorado.

Miss Florence McKinnon was engaged to teach Allan to play the piano. This surprised me, I thought my brother already knew how. The large upright pianoforte stood in a corner of the drawing-room and behind it there was a triangular space that held shelves stacked with music. My mother played and often sang—beautifully—as she did so, *Little Grey Home in the West ... One Day When We Were Young....* But Allan! He drew incredible sounds from the instrument—Chopin! Ravel! Beethoven! And always finishing with his favourites, splendid Sousa marches. I would watch agape as his fingers flew over the keyboard and I would marvel. To think he was **my brother!** And only three years older than me!

I did not realize that the pianoforte was really a pianola ... a magic instrument. You slid open a door at the front and inserted a perforated roll, went to work on the pedals, and something strange happened: Chopin, Ravel and Beethoven poured out. Also splendid Sousa marches. If you were really keen on making idiots of small sisters, you made sure that your fingers flew over the keyboard with panache.

This was all made clear when the news of Miss McKinnon's appointment broke. There was a lot of laughter and cries of 'Fancy you being such a silly girl! Thinking that was him playing!' It was a great joke in The Kitchen.

'Go on, you have a go!' Allan tried to show me how to make the pianola do its magic tricks but my legs were too short and didn't reach the pedals.

Miss McKinnon came once a week. She arrived in mid-morning and left after 4 o'clock tea. The train brought her and she walked down the long dusty road from the outside world wearing a smart dress of flowered material and a straw hat, her music carried in a rafia-embroidered basket. She also wore lisle stockings, the like of which I had never seen before.

I was bidden to keep away from the drawing-room on music lesson days and not hinder my brother's progress. My turn would come. There was practical work in the morning and theory in the afternoon, and I was pleased to discover that Allan couldn't play a thing, let alone Beethoven and Ravel. Not even a splendid Sousa march.

At noon, Miss McKinnon had her breakfast in The Kitchen then went Under-the-House for an hour. She ate separately from the Kitchen for she was not one of them. She was something that I, and they, had never met before—a young, upwardly mobile black woman with not only a trade but a talent. They served her meal at a special table in the kitchen, on a place-mat with a napkin and the cutlery laid out properly. No tinnin plate and spoon, the enamel utensils they used themselves. They called her Miss McKinnon.

Under-the-House she sat in our play area, sometimes on the swing, sometimes on a wicker chair brought down for her. On her first day I went to join her—shyly, for new people did not often come into my world.

She was slight, elfin. A heart-shaped face with high cheekbones, a tiny nose, a pointed chin. Eyes that could suddenly open very wide when she was telling a story. 'Don't humBUG Miss McKinnon!' the Kitchen warned.

But her long fingers beckoned me on the very first day.

'Come,' she said, on that first day. 'Tell me about yourself.'

There was nothing to tell. How could there be? I was a small girl in a small world and when I met new people I had nothing to say. So I just went closer and looked at the pointed face, the questioning eyes, at the young woman who wanted to know about **me**, who actually thought there might be something to know.

I just looked at her.

I did not know I was looking at the person who would show me El Dorado.

As I had nothing to tell her, she told me about Buxton instead, the village on the coast where she lived. A dusty, dreary village. The listening servants had not realized there was anything to know about it. We drove through it on our trips to Georgetown, sometimes stopping on the way back to buy produce.

Buxton produce was renowned along the coast. It was brought to the door from time to time—'Madam! A woman from Buxton bring a fowl!' 'Madam! Is want you want eddoe and yam? A woman from Buxton bring good eddoe and yam!'

The village, she told us, came into being in 1833. That was an historic year, the year when slavery was abolished. At Abolition, the British Government gave the planters £50 for each slave. This laughable sum was meant to make up for losing that slave's labour—laughable for it could not possibly do so. The authorities quickly recognized this fact for the slaves did not get their complete freedom right away. Instead, they were bound to work for their masters for seven more years, and during those seven years they were expected to work for three-quarters of the day. This was even more laughable, it was a badly thought-out scheme that was doomed before it started. The semi-liberated slaves quite naturally did not work as before, if they worked at all, and there was no one to make them do so. There were no longer Drivers with whips on the prowl, ready to slash them for idling. As they saw it, they were already free. No one could bloody their backs with whips now and no one did.

So the old order on the plantations broke down. In a lot of cases the plantations themselves broke down. They simply ceased to operate. Many of them were put up for sale at ridiculous prices and— irony of ironies!—groups of the slaves who had savings actually clubbed together to buy them.

Buxton was the first of these enterprises. They named it after the abolitionist who, a decade before, had tried to bring about laws to make the slaves' lot easier (and so led to an uprising, which made nothing easier). But what to do with the land when they got it? How to support themselves?

The Africans had farmed in their own country of course, and the first influx of slaves tried to do so in Guiana. After nightfall, after a day's work in the canefields. With aching limbs and hungry bellies, in the jumby-ridden dark. In those conditions their efforts were next to fruitless. Nor was this helped by the punishment they got when they were caught cooking in the canefields.

For obvious reasons fires in the canefields were forbidden. A single spark in those dry fields could wipe out an entire crop, a whole year's profits. Forbidden they were, but the slaves made fires all the same, to heat up their Binebyes, the food they took from their homes to eat by-and-by. When they were caught, the punishment went beyond the usual whipping: their 'farms' were flattened and, to make a really good job of it, their livestock was slaughtered. The 'farms' were barely subsistence farms and were usually no more than a few square yards of root crops and corn, which an overseer on a mule could demolish in minutes, while the livestock would have been some fowls or a pig. Not surprisingly, the slaves' will to go on farming withered.

It only withered, it did not die. In the people who bought Buxton it was clearly alive, for more than a hundred years later their produce was still being sold up and down the coast. When you were lucky enough to have a woman from Buxton bring a basket of produce to your door, it was never picked over, never prodded suspiciously and never turned away. It was bought instantly: women from Buxton did not need to peddle their wares.

'Eh-eh! But Miss McKinnon, how you know all this?'

Under-the-House they wondered at her. We truly had never seen anyone like her, anyone so fluent and informed. She listened, she told us, to all that the Old-People said. The Old-People had a lot to say, they had heard all sorts of things—things like how the Colony began and what customs the colonists had brought from their countries and those the slaves themselves brought from Africa—heard it from **their** Old-People who, in turn, had heard it from theirs. In a country like ours, where so many people could not read or write, there were plenty of stories handed down, plenty of word-of-mouth. The Old-People needed to remember, so that those who came after them would know all those things that had happened, so that they would know their history. She had been hearing all their stories and listening to them since she was a little girl. We were lucky to have the Old-People with us, Miss McKinnon stressed, because Old-People's talk was better than newspapers. No, it wasn't all true, she agreed, not all of it. But then, neither were the news-papers.

She didn't only listen—she read. Never throw away old books, she told us, no matter how worm-eaten. The older the books the better because you never knew what you might find in them, especially in a colony where so many people had come from so many different places. Some of the old books they brought with them would have been precious at the time, that was why they had been transported across the world. So—think how much more precious they were now! She had all sorts of people on the look-out for books like that (Mr. Motoo, the pedlar, was one) and now she had quite a collection.

Then she told us how the slaves in Guiana had learned to read.

John Smith and his wife Jane were English missionaries. A kindly couple, welcomed in the Colony at first. But when they announced that they actually planned **to teach the slaves to read** the reaction was one of shock—horror—panic even. The news spread rapidly and the Governor threatened the pair with immediate expulsion from the Colony. This humane—down-right alarming!—attitude to slaves was something new. Noth-ing like it had ever been heard before. **Teach the slaves to read!** Such a scheme was fraught with danger. It was generally agreed that thinking of that sort could destroy not only the sugar trade but the entire colonial way of life. And what would be the effect on the Mother Country? No, slaves were slaves, they needed not even basic education.

Then in 1823 there was a slave uprising. Everyone's fears were confirmed, everyone's predictions had come true: **this was the sort of thing that happened when you taught slaves to read.**

So John Smith was arrested. The charges against him were many, notable among them 'inciting to revolution' and breeding discontent among the slave population. He was tried for these crimes, found guilty, and sentenced to be hanged. Later, a reprieve was granted but alas, John Smith never knew it. He died in prison (not from hanging) before the news could be given to him. Many, many years later, when Guiana was counting its heroes, he became known as Martyr Smith. But when Miss McKinnon told us the story Under-the-House he was still the Englishman the Old-People had talked about, Mr. Smith from the London Missionary Society who with his wife Jane, had taught the slaves in our Colony to read and write. Somewhere in Georgetown there was a Smith Memorial Church.

There was more. The Kitchen was disbelieving when she started telling us about a Governor's Ball that took place in the 18th century, a ball she found recorded in one of her old books. This was no ordinary Ball. It had been held in the grand ballroom at Government House and had been given **for the slaves**.

A long pause for impact.

A doubtful 'Eh-eh! Fo' true—?'

True, she said. It was all written down, in one of her worm-eaten old books that Mr. Motoo, the pedlar, had found for her, the pages so yellowed and fragile she sometimes had to blow on them to turn them (you couldn't handle paper that thin.) The Governor had given a party for the slaves—at Government House!—one historic evening and when night fell they went into the ballroom where a band played. We were all keen to know how the slaves were dressed but she could not tell us. She liked to think of them wearing the kind of clothes their masters and mistresses would have worn to a Ball, she said, and so did we. But whatever they wore would have been brightly coloured and brightly ornamented for sure, for they wore colour to brighten their lives: in their lives the sun was not enough.

What was recorded was that the slaves danced beautifully. Not the tribal dances they had brought from Africa, but the English dances of those days that they had watched time and again, onlookers in the darkness at scenes they could never hope to join. They were especially good, it seemed, at the minuet. The English onlookers were astonished by their knowledge of the dance and the intricacies of the steps, their gracefulness and the fluidity of their movements. Some even said they danced more elegantly than the English!

The Kitchen laughed and laughed when they heard the last part, they were a people who had no doubt at all about their own superiority on the dance floor. They laughed because they knew (of course they knew!) that they had always danced better than their masters.

Miss McKinnon wanted to know about my friends. Like Aunt Marie FitzGerald she seemed to think this was important. So I told her about the de Praslins, who had started life as my dolls, then along the way had come to life and became a family.

They had what I thought were exotic names. Jessica, Viola, Diane. Edward, Teddy and Ned (I had three teddies). They also had a fleet of Rolls Royces, the only car besides Morris that I could name, and stables of horses. The yachts (there were many) were anchored off various Caribbean islands. The de Praslins had adventures in keeping with their background and I played the largest part in all of them.

'Eh-eh! But listen to lies!'

Under-the-House, they gaped. They had never known about the de Praslins.

Miss McKinnon listened keenly and gave a lot of thought to what Jessica should wear to the Garden Party at Buckingham Palace; she cut pictures of dresses out of magazines for Jessica to consider. She knew exactly how Edward, Teddy and Ned could retrieve the yacht stolen by pirates and she also told me about her own friends.

They had strange names. Nicholas Nickleby, Martin Chuzzlewit. Heathcliff. Rochester. Beautiful names: Persephone. Cathy. Emily. Minnie-ha-ha. The places they lived in had strange names too. New Moon. The Shining Big Sea-water. Wuthering Heights, Wildfell Hall. She told me about an old gentleman called Prospero and his daughter, Miranda. A lady called Titania, and her husband Oberon.

Miss McKinnon knew them all and loved telling me about them—dramatically, with significant pauses, much indrawn breath and quick turns to look behind her at imaginary sounds. Her voice fell and rose and quivered at all the right places, her eyes would open wide, her body straighten swiftly and her hands fly up as she gasped—'**All of a sudden**—!'

She was a story-teller without equal. Now I think that she must have come from a long, long line of story-tellers. So much of what she told me was memorable, believable, her word-of-mouth stories heard from the Old-People were every bit as credible and fascinating as the ones she read and recalled. And that I still recall.

What an empty childhood you must have had, people still say to me, all these years later. Stuck out there on a sugar plantation all on your own! A **sugar plantation**, for heaven's sake! No friends to play with, no kindergarten, no television! No dancing class! Only your dolls, your books and your brother!

Poor you!

Not so. I had and I still have the friends I made with Miss McKinnon. Nicholas Nickleby, Martin Chuzzlewit. Minnie-ha-ha. Persephone. Elizabeth Bennet.

All, all of those and many more.

Chapter Eight

Wartime Christmases were memorable for their shortages. Everything we had relied on from abroad was suddenly in short supply. Dried fruit, the most vital ingredient of the famous Guianese Black Cake, was one of them. The supply from the United Kingdom had come to a halt, although many shops and households had had the foresight to hoard large stocks. Aunt Vic held the dried fruit we were sent from England in contempt and was reluctant to give it store-room space. She was convinced that a vast acreage of forgotten warehouses stuffed with dried fruit had once been discovered—and, on the point of destroying the lot, the owners had suddenly thought 'Guiana!' and now sent shiploads to the Colony year after year.

'They think we can't tell good from bad,' she'd say darkly, 'They think we don't notice that every year the dried fruit is worse than the year before. They think we're **ignorant**.'

Thinking someone **ignorant** was the definitive Guianese insult.

In The Kitchen, Christmas preparations began well before December with a ritual known as Setting The Fruit. My mother's recipe book, the Cookery Book—it was the one and only so needed no other definition—was brought out and tucked away inside was an old envelope with the Black Cake Recipe. A yellowed piece of paper now permanently creased, the ingredients and quantities carefully written out in writing so faded—I always meant to ask whose—it had to be held up to the light and spectacles put on to peer at it. (There was also a chapter on how maids should be dressed.)

The fruit, small hard black pellets, showed no promise at this stage. It was weighed and put into enormous glass jars and a great deal of rum was then lavished on it. This was the initial step in the making of the Black Cake and it was fascinating for a small child to watch as the hard little balls slowly began to swell and become recognisable (to The Kitchen) as currants, raisins and sultanas. The origins of this cake are dim but co-lonial kitchens all over the Caribbean have been producing something like it for hundreds of years.

'Shows how long that dried fruit has been hanging about,' Aunt Vic would say when she was reminded of this.

'Vic—it is **dried fruit!**' My mother would try to explain. But it is a fact that it would not have been possible to make any sort of edible cake without soaking the fruit, pellet-hard and pinging when it arrived, in rum for many weeks.

Every family in Guiana had its own Black Cake Recipe and every family's recipe was the **only** true and original one. When recipes were discussed and compared an ingredient vital to that particular recipe would always be left out: the cake-makers didn't share their secrets. I don't remember anyone but Mummy and Aunt Vic seeing our recipe. I copied it once when the original started to fall apart and it was folded and put back in the cookery book, then the original copy was carefully fed to the cast-iron stove. We watched it burn. I was told that the recipe would be mine if I ever learned how to cook, but it never came my way.

Cake-making took place in October. Eggs, a large number of them, had to be collected, and there would be concern if the hens weren't laying. Fresh eggs were a must and no egg was felt to be fresh unless it came from our very own hens. If in-house eggs were not available the word got around; market women came with baskets on their heads and invited Aunt Vic, whose scepticism was known far and wide, to put their eggs in water to see if they would float or not, that well-known test of fresh-ness.

Then the flour had to be examined for weevils, my job which I enjoyed doing, squashing 'the little devils' (Kitchen-speak) under my thumbnail. The butter, which came in tins, would be brought out from the store cupboard to be opened and sampled with suspicion; sometimes it was rancid. Those hurdles crossed, everyone took turns at beating the butter and sugar (always the best brown sugar from the factory) and Joseph came over to lend an arm. The vital ingredients, and all those secret ones, were added with the dried fruit—now soaked in rum and tasting only of rum—the cake tins filled with the batter and put into the oven. Allan and I were then allowed to lick the bowl clean. To me, the Black Cake always tasted better at this stage than it did when cooked. Drizzled generously with rum when still warm from the oven then matured for weeks, during which time it was anointed again and again with yet more rum, the Guianese Black Cake called for a more sophisticated palate than mine.

Aunt Vic sometimes produced a cake using mostly local fruit she had dried herself. This seemed to consist largely of grapefruit peel and pineapple, with an addition of the despised UK export. I used to look forward to this cake, forgetting that with the secret ingredients (some of which turned out to be Angostura Bitters and black molasses) and then impregnated with rum as always, it tasted exactly the same as the Black Cake.

The seasonal drink was Fly (not to be confused with Spanish Fly) which was made from the white sweet-potato and drunk from delicate thimble-sized glasses, children always being obliged to take a sip, like it or loathe it. There was a belief among adults in Guiana (a belief disproved but nevertheless persisted in) that an aversion to alcohol if made in childhood, would last throughout life.

Besides Black Cake, Christmas also meant a visit to the Five-and-Ten, a very successful store where Santa Claus had a grotto and handed out parcels to good children. I always had my doubts about him. It was obvious that his beard and whiskers were made of cotton-wool, but when I finally voiced those doubts to my mother she explained that **of course** he wasn't real! Had I ever thought he was? Silly girl! He was a **substitute**. A stand-in. Everybody knew that! Not even Santa could be all over the world at the same time. Just think about it! He had helpers, of course he had, lots of them. But **somewhere among all those helpers**, was the real Santa Claus—no one ever knew where ... and who knew! Perhaps he would be in the Five-and-Ten next year!

It all made sense to me.

Some time during that season there was a party Under-The-House. An equal number of motherless and fatherless orphans came for cake and lemonade, followed by ice-cream. Then they stood in two rows, the motherless on one side, the fatherless on the other, to receive their presents; why they were segregated I do not know, unless it was to make sure that the adults knew exactly what to say to them. After unwrapping their presents and comparing them, finishing up the ice-cream and cake with a lot of chatter, they went home. Urged to play games they showed no enthusiasm so that line was not pursued.

On the night of Christmas Eve, we were taken to our grandmother's house. Our visits there were always made in daylight so this one, negotiated in the dark and accompanied by Woman Billy with a large flashlight and repeated admonitions to KEEP HOLD OF HER HAND, was exciting. Mother's house was lit by oil lamps, which gave it a magic it never had by day. We had supper there (boiled Guinea fowl eggs which I later discovered were a delicacy in other parts of the world). Afterwards, exactly as the clock struck eight, Woman Billy would say it was time to take us home and Mother would agree. 'Who knows what you two will find there?' she'd say mysteriously, which hurried us on our way. In pre-war days our house smelled of pine when we got there and a real Christmas tree all the way from Canada, already decorated by our parents, glittered before our astonished eyes and reflected back in the highly polished floor.

Colonial kitchens cooked a traditional English Christmas dinner. They had always done so and they would cook no other. They had been programmed since the English colonists raised the flag on new territory and they would not have dreamed of doing anything else. That was the way things were done. Suggestions for a simple meal with everything prepared the day before for my mother and Aunt Vic to put in the oven so that The Kitchen could take the day off were always met with disbelief and opposition if not downright hilarity That was **not** the way things were done and that was that.

The oven was always too hot or too cold on Christmas Day. The Kitchen fussed, Aunt Vic fussed, my mother looked on with carefully contained despair, Joseph put on his white coat with brass buttons to serve the meal and brought in the flaming pudding with a flourish. Everyone enjoyed the day—the bigger the disaster that threatened in The Kitchen the more enjoyable it seemed—and as my father frequently said when we ate our piping hot dinner on that unfailingly sultry Christmas Day, it would have been unthinkable to deprive them of all that fun. Especially at Christmas.

A few hand-picked overseers would be invited for lunch. This was before the Club House was built; until then the young men had nowhere to go and made up their own parties in the Overseers' Quarters, where there seemed to be plenty of drink but never enough food. The new overseers were always invited— 'so far from home' was my mother's kindly thought—and the numbers varied, sometimes two or three, sometimes just one. I remember few of the invitees, there always seemed to be so many of them.

There was one I never forgot. The solitary new overseer was in an obvious hurry to get through his meal. We children defeated him by taking our time. Finally, replete with roast turkey and all that went with it, Christmas pudding, imported tinned cream—and of course rum—he turned to my mother, on saying goodbye, and told her, 'Thank you Mrs. Winter, that was very good. Adding—'But, say what you like, there is nothing like an English Christmas!'

My mother wept that night. He was young, Daddy pointed out, he had probably never been out of England before, had not had a good upbringing, did not know his P's and Q's.…Mummy would hear none of it and vowed she would never ask any of those young men to Christmas lunch again. Never again. She meant it, she said firmly. Never!

The next Christmas she seemed to have forgotten her vow. The new overseers were invited as usual. The one who had been in a hurry the year before, had been keen to get back to his carousing buddies and join the drinking. It turned out that alcohol was a new experience for him, the demon drink was never allowed in his parents' home.

The grown-ups seemed to find that amusing.

* * *

A few weeks before Easter the sky became busy with kites. Kites of all colours and sizes bobbed and ducked and spun and soared, whirled in crazy circles and frequently plunged to the ground to be smashed beyond repair. Allan and I flew our kites at Easter and not one day before. Running to Mummy and pointing out all the bright kites already bobbing and weaving in the sky, with pleas of 'Look—everyone's flying their kites already—why can't we fly ours?' got us nowhere. Her rules were not made for bending. The kite-fliers, she reminded us every year, were probably Muslims or Buddhists or one of the many other religions in the Colony, who did not realise that the flying of kites was a symbol of the Resurrection and should on no account be done before Easter Day, let alone before Lent.

We had to be satisfied with making our kites. This was not as simple as it sounds. There was no question of going to the shops and buying the materials we needed. The shops were far away, eighteen whole miles away in Georgetown. Adults who wanted dressmaking fabrics and small children anxious for shiny kite-paper and yards of string were all at the mercy of the estate messenger, an East Indian called Bechu Lal who made weekly visits to town on the train and sometimes did the shopping if he had time and sometimes did not.

He frequently turned up from his shopping forays without the vital paper and string. We didn't dare complain. He was the estate Man-of-Business, indispensable to all the ladies and **on no account** was he to be upset or even allowed to **suspect** how disappointed we were. Small children's kite materials were not high on the list of vital necessities.

Eventually what we needed would appear, usually minus the large pot of paste with a brush. This was a luxury, difficult to find. Great care was taken of the paste-pot when we did manage to get one, such great care that the paste was usually hard and useless by the time we opened it. We tried to make do with flour paste but usually someone would turn up with a bunch of glamma cherries. These are an inedible fruit with amazing stickability, the green equivalent of superglue.

Allan's kites were splendid affairs, they were large and glittering, they soared and sang and were things of beauty.

Grownups seemed to enjoy helping him make his kites and suggesting even better ways of decorating them and talking about things called aerodynamics. Mine were put together with less enthusiasm.

On Easter Day we picnicked at Hope Beach, a few miles farther along the coast. It was not the white stretch of sand and sparkling sea that the word 'beach' suggests. Guiana is on a mud shelf that stretches miles out to sea, so the sea itself is a drab beige colour. It is full of a fine silt and anyone putting their head right under the water comes up again with their hair lightly coated with this silt. It is because of this that Guianese are known in the Caribbean as 'mudheads'.

It follows that the beach is also mud-coloured. Why that particular one was called Hope Beach I never knew. At first sight it seemed a dreary place from which all hope had gone. Empty tins lay about and broken coconut shells. Two sisters had drowned there; small East Indian boys were always waiting, ready to point to the spot. Even the coconut palms were straggly and lacking in the glamour of the tropical palm. Some of them had been decapitated in strong winds, fruit and fronds flying off, leaving only the tall thin trunks standing desolate against the sky. A place entirely without hope. We loved it.

At Easter the picnic hamper was brought out from the back of the storeroom. It could not be opened in the house because having laid dormant and unused for a whole year it had become a refuge for mini-wildlife. Taken downstairs and the lid thrown open, I could imagine spiders, centipedes, scorpions and other creepy crawlies as yet unnamed by etymologists rushing out of it. Terrified of scuttling things, I would stay upstairs listening to The Kitchen inhabitants running around and yelling as they swatted the horrors. 'It's supposed to be cleaned out regularly!' my mother would remind them, 'Let's not have this happen again next year!' It always did.

The hamper was transformed when packed for the picnic, wicker lined with green baize and full of interesting compartments which held their own picnic plates and cutlery, bottles and cocktail shakers. It produced egg sandwiches, corned beef sandwiches, lemonade, gin-and-tonic for adults, and hot green-leaf tea out of a thermos, cakes of all kinds and, best of all, the meat patties Aunt Vic made from a recipe that I have searched the world's cookery books for since and have never found.

The kites had to be launched right away, we'd waited long enough. This was the point at which, each year, I re-discovered why no one was keen to help me make mine. Allan's kite seemed to take to the air effortlessly and usually without adult help, it soared higher and higher and dazzled everyone with its bright decorations and its technical expertise. Admiring observers asked him, 'You mek that? Eh-eh! You mek it good!'

Mine, on the other hand, seldom flew. Rejecting help, I'd run along the beach with it, convinced that it was taking flight behind me, elated that I had cracked the secret of kite-launching—only to realize when I was joined by a straggle of small boys jumping and jeering alongside, that the kite I'd put together with such hope had become a sad object dragged to tatters behind me.

It must have been laughable to watch, and not only because of the little girl with her kite on a long string thumping and bumping behind her. For reasons I didn't know then and don't know now, small East Indian boys in the country districts wore nothing but shirts. Sometimes small shirts, sometimes large shirts, but never buttoned, always hanging loosely with shirttails flapping. As they ran the shirts streaked out behind them, their naked brown bodies totally exposed, little penises jiggling, balls bobbing briskly. Unfortunately, I was so used to the sight I did not realise how funny they looked until I grew up; if I had I would have turned and done some jeering myself. But I doubt if they would have known why.

Later in the day, a wicked game began. Sinister kites hitherto unseen rose up from behind clumps of vegetation, their fliers hidden, their sole objective to bring down other kites. The bigger and better and more beautiful the kite, the more quickly they spotted it and moved in for the attack. It did not help to run farther along the beach, you would be pursued and would not know who was doing the pursuing: the attacking kite would be all that was visible. Sometimes they simply wrapped their strings around yours and both kites would plunge to the ground and be lost. At other times the game was more skilful, the skilled players identified by their kite-tails which glinted with razor blades, out to slash and destroy.

It was riveting to sit and watch the battles going on in the sky, as long as it wasn't your kite that was being attacked. That was Allan's fear, mine was that the slasher kite would get out of control, fly close to earth and slash **me**. It seemed entirely possible.

When the afternoon cooled, we packed up to go home. That was when the small East Indians boys who had been jeering at me and who by then I loathed passionately, appeared from behind trees and clumps of tall grass and stood around on one foot, scratching a skinny leg with the other, all looking pitiful. Deprived and ill-fed. This filled me with helpless fury. I'd had my share of cakes and patties and I knew that The Kitchen over-catered for just this purpose ('There are always some small boys there, they run with Pam and encourage her—') but I couldn't bear to see my mother handing out the leftovers. These were the very boys who had run beside me and my little kite that had never flown, mocking, taunting, jumping up and down, imitating me, pointing and jeering at me when I lost my temper or worse, burst into tears.

Now, they mocked me still with swift darting looks, as they advanced circumspectly to my mother, hands outstretched, faces radiant with the innocence of childhood.

I flounced angrily off to the car.

'Now you come back here and pick your kite up,' I would be told, 'Don't leave litter lying around.'

Tajah and Pagwah sounded very much alike but were vastly different. These were both festivals connected with East Indian religions, and from year to year I only remembered that I was called to look at and admire one, but instructed to stay away, far away from the other—not just stay far away but to keep indoors and not even go Under-the-House while Pagwah was going on.

The Tajah was an edifice carried by the Muslims when they celebrated one of their holy days. This particular day, and the Tajah edifice, commemorated the killing of Hussein, the son of a holy man. Hussein had been slain on a holy site, a site so remote that followers could not visit it. So the edifices were made to represent his tomb and carried shoulder-high so all could see. Each plantation held its own festival, and days in advance we would hear calls of 'They buildin' the Tajah!' Help from the community in general was offered and accepted and when the cry changed to 'The Tajah comin'!' the procession could be glimpsed in the distance. The Kitchen, which previously professed disinterest, crowded at the windows and always made sure I had a good position. The procession usually went by our house but once, and it is an occasion that is carved in memory, the leaders decided to come to our back gate. They must have known of our pop-eyed wonder. Our parents forestalled this and the procession was diverted to the front gate to show respect for another religion, another culture. The gallery was long with many windows and was able to hold more spectators than The Kitchen.

The Tajah was large and high and, carried on shoulders, it seemed to be floating above the procession. The leaders stopped outside the front gate and turned to face the house, the Tajah resplendent above them. It glittered in the sun, to my child's eyes it seemed to be made of pure gold and encrusted with precious jewels.

'You must thank them,' Mummy told me, 'They stopped here especially for you and Allan, so that you could see.'

I stood by the door and mouthed my thanks which they could have neither seen nor heard. It was the best I could do as I became suddenly shy, so aloof and so dignified, so different all the men looked in their robes. I could not believe they were the same people who worked in the fields and factory and gave me a cheerful greeting whenever they saw me and always said 'Salaam' (peace) to my father.

Then I suddenly thought of curtseying, which I was teaching myself to do in case I ever went to Buckingham Palace to be presented at Court. (This always amused Mummy and Daddy,

I could never think why.) I took centre stage at the wide front door, and performed my version of the curtsey, which I had only seen in books. Skirt held out on both sides—right foot very straight in front—pointy toes ... a wide semi-circle slowly traced with the foot, still pointy ... and then a deeper, slower bow. Very deep and very slow ... held for as long as I could. I remembered to smile as I straightened up.... There was a gasp from the crowd and a deep murmur of appreciation—then they broke into loud cheering and clapping. My mother was delighted.

There was a glow in the sky that night. 'They are burning the Tajah' I was told. But I did not want to believe it, I could not believe that such a beautiful object could be so laboriously made and then so deliberately destroyed.

'They will make another one next year,' I was told, 'It might be even better, you'll see.'

And they did, the cry of 'Tajah comin'' went up as before; The Kitchen crowded by the windows to watch and I watched with them. But the Tajah never came so close to the house again and never stopped outside the front gate.

Pagwah was hugely different. It was a high-spirited Hindu festival that embraced all creeds and colours, to the dismay of those embraced. In olden days in India it is said to have taken as long as a month to celebrate. Thankfully, by the time it reached Guiana it had become a three-day event. Days before it started there would be a lot of visiting, strange women in bright saris could be seen flitting about, whole families from other plantations or villages, even from Georgetown, would appear with small children being pulled along looking uncomfortable in new shoes and white socks, on the way to visit other families. A frenzy of cooking went on and I always hoped to be invited to someone's house, but if there was an invitation I never heard of it.

When we were told to stay indoors we knew the high point of Pagwah had come. My father put on his oldest jacket, the one Mummy was always about to throw out before she remember about Pagwah; the Kitchen left their working clothes behind the night before and turned up in any old thing.

On that day, a day eagerly awaited by the younger Hindu population, they threw coloured water (usually red) on each other and on anyone else going about their business, smeared coloured powder (any colour) on them, and a lucky few who had managed to get balloons filled them with coloured water and whacked them about indiscriminately. The children filled tubs with red water and jumped in or threw each other in, a practice the adults discouraged ('One of these days one of you picknie will drown good!') A lot of people ended the day brightly coloured, happy to be so and to tell friends how they had been caught out.

This was said to be a cleansing ritual after the winter and a welcome to the new season, but as the only seasons in Guiana were Rainy and Dry, this part of it was largely forgotten. The spreading of good-will was also a part of the festival, and most people seemed quite happy to put on their oldest clothes and join in the spirit of the day. The few who were caught unawares grumbled. Grumbling was about all they could do. It was a day for the Mule Boys and Houseboys to take revenge on the over-seers—the same overseers who would be reminded by authority well in advance that Pagwah was *a religious festival*—that the red water represented the blood of Homulcar and, above all, that the customs and religion of another culture were to be *respected* and, like it or not, *they had to put up with it.*

A disenchanted few were frequently heard to marvel at the number of conversions to Hinduism that conveniently took place that day, people who were known to be Holy Rollers or Jehovah's Witnesses, seemed to feel free to join their Hindu friends.

Diwali, the Festival of Lights, was another holy festival. In some parts of India it was said to be a spectacular affair, a sight never to be forgotten. This festival celebrated the story of Rama and Sita, a prince of the realm and his beautiful wife, who were exiled into the forest because a jealous stepmother wanted her son to be king. In the forest, Sita was kidnapped by a wicked man who wished her beauty for himself. A famous battle to rescue her then took place. Hanuman the Monkey god and General of the Monkey Army, fought for the royal pair.and memorably distinguished himself. Everyone was slain except Hanuman. Magical herbs restored Sita and Rama to life, administered by none other than Hanuman himself.

So they returned to their kingdom.

On hearing of their journey back, a poor woman put a lamp in her window to light the royal pair on their way. Then, magically it seemed, every window in the kingdom became alight as every lamp was lit. The magnificent palace glowed—then the night sky itself seemed ablaze—then, as legend tells it, the whole world was alight as never before or since.

I never saw the Festival of Diwali. It took place at night when, being very young, I would have been fast asleep. Had I known how short a time I was to have in Guiana, I would have urged the grownups to wake me.

But they had seen Diwali many times throughout their lives and it was nothing out of the ordinary to them. They may well have been asleep themselves.

Chapter Nine

Guiana called itself a Nation of Six Peoples and did so with much pride. Justifiably. We lived peacefully, all Six Peoples, at ease with ourselves and at ease with each other, enjoying the country we lived in, taking pride in our city of Georgetown—acknowledged then to be one of the world's loveliest wooden cities with its wide avenues and brilliant blossoming trees; taking pride in the hinterland which would one day be opened up but which in the meantime we called The World's Last Frontier; in the canals, the rivers and creeks, the open skies and the warmth, the colourful people and their different cultures. Above all, we enjoyed our happy hospitality to each other and to strangers.

There were undercurrents, of course. The Colony's history was one of good times and bad. In the 1930s the effects of the Depression were felt in Guiana, manufactured goods and spare parts, textiles and leather goods were in short supply. It was said that the reason they were in short supply was because most people were too poor to buy them so they were never even ordered.

During World War II, shops ran out of basic necessities like strong flour for bread, so in our house cassava bread was substituted. This could be bought from the market women, but only if we knew it had been made in a clean kitchen and the market woman (clean herself) could vouch for it. No one ever forgot that our older sister had died from typhoid fever: this had left my mother and Aunt Vic paranoid about cleanliness, their paranoia was like a virus, it infected the whole Kitchen.

Market woman after market woman came to the back door and was rejected and finally Aunt Vic with a toss of the head and a suck of the teeth (known as suck-teeth or stewpsing-she-teeth) announced that if **that** was the best those women could do, she would make her own. There was disbelief—consternation—in The Kitchen.

'But Miss Vic, you know how long cassava bread tek to mek?'

'Is not something you can mek in this kitchen, you know, is an Aborigine kitchen you want for that!'

'Is not like mekkin bread, Miss Vic! It only **call** bread!'

This was true. Cassava bread was hard, flat and pancake-shaped, fibrous and gritty with a sandpaper-like texture and tasted of nothing at all. It was certainly nor bread as we knew it.

Another toss of the head. If the Aborigines could do it so could Aunt Vic, in fact anything anyone could cook she could cook better. She was convinced of it.

So were most people but it was now suspected that she had overreached herself. Cassava bread was the preserve of the Aboriginal Indians and, according to The Kitchen, entire settlements were press-ganged to work at making it. The cassava tuber was first grated, then squeezed to extract the poisonous juices, then dried—a long, laborious process, they all knew.

'An' **where** we goin' to get a matupi from?' they asked in triumph.

The matupi (pronounced matu-pee in The Kitchen) was a long, thin woven container used to squeeze the grated cassava, not an item you picked up in shops but made only by the Aborigines. If one was not found, then that would be the end of Aunt Vic's grand scheme.

The matupi was found (Mr. Motoo, the pedlar, was said to have been responsible). The cassava was grated, squeezed then dried and cooked, the end product very like today's crispbread but much crisper, and more interesting when eaten warm and dripping with honey. Some agreed that it really was like eating coarse sandpaper but those are people who never ate Aunt Vic's cassava bread (warm and dripping with honey).

That was not all. The poisonous juices were about to be thrown away by the Kitchen when Aunt Vic called a halt. She announced that **she was going to make her own casareep.** All she had to do was boil it down to the right consistency, she said, and lo—casareep!

There was horror in the kitchen. Indrawn breath.

Silence.

They were well aware that this was the accepted procedure but none of them would ever have dreamed of doing it and the words 'poisonous juices' seemed to hover in visible thought bubbles above their heads. Quiet reasoning, protestations, the folding of aprons, putting on of hats and walking out of the Kitchen and down the back steps—the upraised arms and shrieks once the departees had clanged out of the back yard—it was all to no avail.

Aunt Vic did it. She boiled the casareep down to what must have been the right consistency and the end product was judged to look like casareep and, yes—it tasted like casareep. It sat in a dark bottle on a shelf and I think it must have been used. At any rate the bottle seemed to empty gradually, the way casareep bottles did, and we all lived.

During World War II, we had the advantage of an American air base outside Georgetown at Atkinson Field; the Americans employed a large number of Guianese and goodies of every description overflowed from their PX to many parts of the Colony.

It was during one of the good spells that the new factory was built at Enmore. Its skeleton frame rose outside the old building, embracing it and finally swallowing it up. For a time the new factory was the jewel in the Bookers' crown and people came from near and far to be shown around it—from other plantations, from Georgetown and from England. My father enjoyed taking visitors on these conducted tours, he was proud of the new factory, we all were. The old grey structure of the smaller factory became a memory and all that remained of it were its old grey gates. They seemed small and shabby and out of keeping with the splendid new building behind them. They would be replaced, we were told, when everything in the factory was completed and all the new machinery finally in place.

At last it happened. The new gates, taller, wider and larger all over were hung in place, the finishing touch of a grand new project—and the start of a brand new era, the people of Enmore said proudly. Hard-working, illiterate or semi-literate people, the majority of them reasonably happy though materially lacking, people who strove to educate their children so that life would be better for those children; people who sincerely believed that things really would get better. Not for them, they acknowledged that it was too late for them, they'd had no education, but most certainly for their children, everything would be very much better for the next generation. The new factory was seen as a symbol of progress, a move towards better things a better life, a better world. A libation at the gates was talked of: it may have taken place while I was away at school.

They were not to know that those gates would become infamous throughout the Colony. In 1948 during riots—unheard of during my father's 35 years at Enmore—five East Indian men were shot and killed in front of the factory. The ghastly scene was spoken of for years afterwards—the blood of those five men splattered all over the bright white gates.

The background to this story belongs to history. It happened after we had left Enmore, after my father died. A few people turned up at our back door in Georgetown to tell the tale, including Mr. Motoo the pedlar, but each one told a slightly different tale. All they agreed on was the names of the men who died.

The dispute that prompted this disturbance—strike—subsequent riot—was the cane-cutters' demands to change their method of working from Cut-and-Load to Cut-and-Drop. The former method meant that the cutters not only had to cut the cane, they then had to pick it up and load the heavy bundles on the punts which took it to the factory. This was not an historical method, it was introduced in 1945. Imagination fails when trying to picture what it must have been like to cut, drop, pick up, gather up, then load the heavy bundles of sugar cane all daylong in that hellish heat … whereas the Cut-and-Drop method meant that the cutters dropped the cane, to be picked up by other workers who would then load the punts. This would have involved hiring more paid labour and the Management would not agree to it.

There had been many strikes to demand change, but this particular one was organized by the leaders of the newly formed Guiana Industrial Workers Union, which included many rising young politicians, among them one called Cheddi Jagan. It began in April 1948 and went on for weeks, dramatically affecting sugar production. Other issues, every bit as important, were higher wages and better living conditions, but the main reason was to have the new Union acknowledged as the negotiating Union for factory and field workers on all the Guianese sugar plantations.

In June, a picket/protest/demonstration was organized to take place outside the new factory at Enmore. As well as being protected by the locked gates, the factory was doubly protected by a vicious barbed wire fence which rose high around the compound. The Management felt they could not deal with the situation and asked for police help; they were sent six armed policemen led, unbelievably, by a Lance Corporal. When the crowd, now numbering hundreds, found they could not get into the factory, they turned on the police—stones and sticks and broken bottles, anything that could be hurled was hurled, and rioting swiftly broke out. The few policemen could not hold back the rioters and fired on them.

Five men were killed and fourteen injured.

The joint funerals of the dead took place the next day: in tropical heat burial must be swift. The coffins were carried from Enmore to Le Repentir cemetery in Georgetown, the fellow workers of the five men gathered in hundreds throughout the night to accompany them. It is the popular belief among Guianese that on the journey to Le Repentir they were led by Cheddi Jagan. Jagan was the son of an estate Driver (a leader of the gangs who worked in the fields and a person of some authority) and he was one of the rising young politcians. This belief has seeped into Guianese folklore because of the iconic figure that Jagan later became. The people, understandably, liked to think that it was a man like that who, at a time like that, led them into history. They were, in fact, led by already established politicians and dignitaries: Cheddi Jagan was indeed prominent among the crowds, he moved among them and comforted them throughout that dreadful day, and in so doing became their rock—on that day and in all the days and years that followed. Jagan always said that it was on that day that he made the momentous vow to release his people from the bonds of colonialism.

He was later to become Premier of Guiana.

The crowd of thousands could be heard coming from a great distance, it was said; they numbered thousands then, as they were joined by workers from other plantations along the coast. It was not the sound of marching feet that was heard, but a strange shuffling sound—most of the marchers did not have shoes. They were not allowed to proceed through the city as originally planned but were diverted by the police to take a different route.

The police were headed by an Inspector with a machine gun.

It was a day—a sight—a time in our history—that would be seared forever into the soul of our Colony.

The inevitable Investigation followed, a Commission was appointed headed by a Supreme Court Judge and two others. The organisers of the strike and the officials of the Union did not testify; they felt the Commission would find in favour of the Police and the plantation Management. So they did. The policemen claimed they opened fire to save damage to the factory and the lives of the workers inside. But in spite of finding in their favour, the Commission went on to criticise them for not using tear gas to disperse the crowds and for shooting 'beyond the requirements of the situation … some others received shots when in actual flight.' One, indeed, was shot in the back.

A multitude of men set out that day in June hoping to make a change. Five men were killed and many lives were changed.

Some of those changes came rapidly, some like living conditions, more slowly. But change there was and not only for the workers and not only in the basics like better pay and living conditions. Change came, very importantly, in negotiations with management: it used to be said that 'Massa don' listen' which later became 'Massa don' hear' then 'Massa he got no ears.' From then on Massa heard and what was more, Massa took action.

Change came further up the hierarchy in the social life of the plantations. Guianese girls who had married overseers lived their lives in the compound, looking after their small children or working in Georgetown and socialising among themselves. Now, they were invited to coffee mornings by the Managers' wives and to Sunday drinks in the Managers' houses. English staff being driven to town had always done so in the back seat, properly dressed like proper colonials in white shirt and tie—now, they sat beside the driver, tie-less and with opened collar.

As for the Managers themselves! Some of them were very august personages indeed who had always worn stiffly starched breeches in dazzling white—similar jackets with long sleeves (God help them in that heat) shimmering riding boots and shining swagger sticks (why the latter I never knew) and brilliant white solar topee ... these personages were requested to dress down. Later, there came a time when local overseers were promoted to Management, some became Managers of plantations themselves.

These instructions had come from Head Office in London. Democracy had come to Guiana.

Colonialism was dying fast.

Without that ghastly slaughter that took place at Enmore, it was generally recognised that these changes would have been a great deal slower in coming. The deaths of the men were the catalyst. The martyrdom of those men were recognised in 1976, at the Continental Council of the National Affiliates of the World Peace Council in Bogota, Colombia.

At Enmore, where they died, a memorial stands to them. Their names are inscribed:

LALLABAGEE KISSOON (30 years old, shot in the back)
POORAN (Aged 19, shot in the back and pelvis)
RAMBARRAN (Died from bullet wounds in his leg)
DOOKHIE (Died of his wounds in hospital that day)
HARRY (Died the following day from severe spinal injuries)

These five men are known as The Enmore Martyrs.

Chapter Ten

My mother held strong views about marriage: couples who lived together should be married and couples with children should quite definitely be married. It was a view held by many ladies at that time, a time when cohabiting was known as Living in Sin and illegitimacy, in that part of the world, was a common state. In the Caribbean islands, marriage-conscious Governors' wives and other worthy ladies organized mass marriages of white-haired grandparents and great-grandparents, the descendants of slaves who had no tradition of marriage. These frail old folk tottered or were carried to open-air altars to make their quavering vows and be photographed in their best clothes by *Life* magazine.

My mother did her bit whenever she got the chance, urging young people to marry. The East Indians married and their elders liked to keep up the pretence that those marriages were arranged, as they would have been in India. Early arranged marriages were frowned upon by the authorities and by the 1930s the custom had died out. Meetings between young people were always being engineered by family and friends who could then say, if the couple fell in love and married, that it had been 'arranged'. Everyone would be happy and agree that the old ways were the best.

Inter-racial marriages were not encouraged and when they did happen there was a certain element of scepticism about their viability. The East Indian weddings were glittering affairs that went on for days with much ceremony and feasting, their impoverished dwellings and the people themselves transformed. The weddings must have cost thousands and everyone marvelled at them, the greatest marvel being how all that money had been found.

Woman Billy took Allan and me to a wedding once. The bride, Susan, worked in the Wood Gang, she was one of the girls who carried firewood to feed the stoves of the staff houses.

The red logs were piled in large round baskets balanced on a thick coil of rolled cotton laid flat on the girls' heads, one hand raised to hold the basket, the other held out sideways and moving rhythmically, like a paddle. The water-carriers also walked like this. They all swayed as they walked and were a lovely sight especially when there were two or more of them walking together, or sometimes a whole line of them.

Susan brought our wood regularly and was popular in The Kitchen. She walked sedately, was bare-footed and bangled, and had lustrous black hair. Masses of it. Her face was beautiful. And she wore her faded old clothes for work which was commendable: Susan was said to Know Her Place. The African girls who wore bright clothes, flashed their teeth and eyes and swayed seductively were girls who Did Not Know Their Place. They caused young heads to turn, old heads to shake. No good would come to them, it was said, no good at all. The fact that quite a few made good in one way or another and ended up wearing even brighter clothes, did not kill this belief.

Susan's wedding was held in the Indian section of the range dwellings. The room glittered. The guests glittered. A great deal of gold was on show. I looked around eagerly for the bride and could not believe that the silk-clad beauty who stood beside the bridegroom, the handsome dark, yes, glittering bridegroom, was Susan. The guests were themselves splendid in their best saris, and jewellery, the men in white sharkskin suits, but Susan and her bridegroom outshone them. They stood apart from the rest like beings from some distant starship, golden, glowing.

'Look the flies!' Woman Billy said, 'Eh eh! Who ever see so many flies! You children don' eat anything, you hear? They vomit quick,' she explained to people who kept pressing food on us, delicious-looking treats that were hastily whipped away.

Flies there were, but we were used to them. Neither they nor Woman Billy or even being denied that sumptuous-looking food and the exotic sweets we were dying to gorge on, could spoil that day. It was the day I learned that range dwellings could be changed into palaces—that handsome princes **did** exist and that barefoot girls **could** become princesses. The day I knew that fairy tales really did come true.

The Africans opted out of weddings. They couldn't afford it, they argued. They couldn't afford the rum of which enormous quantities were needed, they couldn't afford the wedding-cake (that rum-soaked edifice), the food, and the new clothes. The man's suit had to be a good one for not only was he to marry in it, he was expected to be buried in it. So marriage was an expensive step and until couples could afford it they simply lived together and had their children and grandchildren and thought no more about it.

Woman Billy was married. Everyone knew this and for this she was held in high regard by my mother. It was very likely one of the points in her favour when she was employed. What my mother did not know was that Woman Billy was married to the Devil.

I had always thought she was married to Man Billy. He was a high, wide, good-looking six-footer, acknowledged by all to be her husband.

'Billy, how yo' husband?' Younger women would enquire in soft voices. A sour look would be the answer—a long suck-teeth, eyes cast up. They would turn away with a smile on their lips, a secret look on their faces.

Then I heard the whispered conversations, the ones I wasn't supposed to hear, usually on our afternoon walks.

'Going for a walk and come back' was Woman Billy's way of describing this sortie, which almost always took us up the long, empty red-dust road that lead out of Enmore. A road that was considered 'safe', so long, so wide and so empty it was.

But Woman Billy and I knew that the Devil lurked there. So did The Kitchen. 'Pray God you don' meet the Devil!' they would call as we clanged out of the gate. There were days when she acknowledged their words with a toss of the head, other days with the usual suck-teeth. Soon, she would start glancing nervously around, she seemed to expect Lucifer to materialise out of the red dust itself.

Her mood was catching. I, too, would look furtively over my shoulder or stare hard at the empty distance, fully expecting to see Satan and his minions marching towards us brandishing torches of fire.

'What you see? What you see?' she would ask anxiously, not believing my repeated answer of 'Nothing.' There was, in truth, nothing to see.

Sometimes we'd be approached by solitary figures, women who clearly knew about the Devil for they oozed sympathy even from a distance, both hands outspread.

'Girl, is HOW?'

The eyes rolling heavenward. The sigh. 'If I tell you what that Devil try to do to me last night—!'

They'd edge away from me. Mutter-mutter. . .

A shrill cry from one of them. 'But look wickedness! I bury three husbands and I tell you, not one of them ever try to do a thing like that to me!'

Clucks of sympathy were heard all round, advice about crosses to bear sent by an all-knowing God, even suggestions that the Devil might one day see the error of his ways.

'Thank the Lord you got a good job,' was often repeated. 'At least the Devil can't touch you there.'

I found this last bit reassuring. It was good to know that our house and all who were in it were out of the Devil's reach.

The Devil played a large part in Woman Billy's conversations and I did not doubt for a moment that she knew him well. She had some devilish tricks herself. She had ways of shutting me up when I wanted to rush home and tell who I'd seen, if anyone at all, and what they'd said, if anything, on our walks. Making sure that when she said 'Do' and 'Don't', I did and I didn't.

All nannies have their methods. Unless children are physically harmed, parents don't know or don't want to know. Woman Billy's method must have been unique: she pretended to shove black hairy spiders down my knickers. The leaping and screaming that followed she watched in straight-faced silence. When at last I managed to tear my knickers off, to find no hairy black spider, it was reported to my mother as 'running around without her knickers, and in front of everyone, Madam.'

Such wickedness was punished by making me wear **two** pairs of knickers—not only very hot and uncomfortable as knickers were then elasticated at both waist and legs and voluminous as well and made of sturdy material—and even better for trapping hairy black spiders.

'You see what happen to bad children? The spiders want to punish you for what you do to me last week!'

'What did I do, Billy?'

It must be said that I was not a blameless charge. Life must have been hell for the poor woman, what with the Devil and his wickedness at night, and me to torment her by day.

'Remember when you pick up that whole cake of dry cow-dung and throw it at my clean white apron that I starched so good? And it turned out the cow-dung was only dry on the outside? And it go plop and splash and make a mess all over me? That's what the spiders punishing you for!'

Why, I have been asked, didn't I simply tell my mother? Or why didn't Allan expose these crimes against me? The reasons were many. When Allan came on our walks there always seemed to be things to do and see and talk about—ant-hills to be leapt over, the kind, according to him, that swarmed with flesh-eating ants that could strip little girls to the bare bones in seconds … the famous one-horned bull (known to all as One Horn, even to this day) to keep an eye on just in case he suddenly charged, to rip and shred us.… But Allan was older than I and long past the nannying stage, his walks with us grew less and less frequent. As for telling my mother—!

We lived in a culture and at a time when adults were held to be **always right**. It did not matter what their status, their race, colour, creed or relationship with the family, or even their mental state. Simply **being adult** made them Right. If adults took it into their heads to complain about a child, no one dreamed of doubting them. If the child had the presumption to actually protest, it was then guilty not only of the alleged crime but of lack of respect as well. **Eye-pass**. Under conditions like these it was easier for little girls (like me) to just shut up and hurl cow-dung.

I had grown so used to all this talk of the Devil that it never occurred to me that my mother might not know about him. All was revealed to her—though not to me—very early one morning (Joseph was still chopping the firewood). I suddenly heard Woman Billy shrieking all the way up the stairs to my parents' bedroom—she actually burst into the bedroom, an unheard-of thing to do. (Everyone was supposed to rap on the door and **wait** before entering, even though the door was kept wide open, day and night) her voice was high and distorted, and when I rushed in to see what was going on, she looked distorted too. Her usually crisp, starched clothes clung to her crookedly, she looked like someone under water. Then I realized why—she had actually **been** under water. Very recently. It was still running off her on to my mother's precious Chinese rug—in drips, in rivulets, and in occasional gushes. The story she told was so terrible that no one even saw what was happening to the rug.

She was telling a tale about the Devil. Had he, I wondered, succeeded in doing that awful thing to her last night, something she frequently complained about in those whispered conversations? But no—the Devil hadn't even shown up. He'd been out all night with that Witch. Or perhaps it was that Bitch…. Woman Billy was so worried, she got up before dawn to look for him.

They met on the hump-backed wooden bridge over a canal, she and the Devil. These bridges were hump-backed to let punts loaded with cane pass under them, so the hump itself, which was where Woman Billy and the Devil met, was fairly high off the water.

'Where you been?' she demanded. 'You got me worrying! What you been doing, out all night?'

'What I been doing?' He seemed very pleased with himself. 'I'll show you what I been doing! I don't need to tek you home either, I going to show you right here 'pon this bridge! Right here, woman!'

She could see from the look in the Devil's eye that he meant it. Right there 'pon that bridge was where he said he'd do it, **and right there 'pon that bridge** was where he meant to do it. There was only one thing for a woman of virtue to do.

She jumped off the high, hump-backed bridge into the canal. The Devil, knowing full well she couldn't swim, just stood there and laughed while she floundered and spluttered and somehow got to the bank … just stood and laughed, expecting to watch her drown. Woman Billy wept all the way to our house and up the stairs to my parents' bedroom.

She stood on the Chinese rug weeping hysterically and my mother made calming noises while Daddy went downstairs to find hot coffee. When I questioned the grown-ups about it later I was told sternly that Woman Billy's affairs were no concern of mine. I was only a child. That evening I heard my mother say to Daddy that if this sort of thing went on, then clearly Billy was not a suitable person to be in charge of the children and what a pity they hadn't known about it before they employed her. My father agreed and said that he would have a word with Man Billy, who worked in the factory. I could not understand what Man Billy had to do with it and my questions were shushed away.

After that, things quietened down. No more was heard of the Devil. It was some time before I came to realise that Man Billy and the Devil were one and the same person. At some stage of this tale I must have laughed out loud, for later there was a memorable lecture from my mother about not laughing at the misfortunes of others. She never knew about Woman Billy's expertise at getting her own back. Another Billy-threat soon followed this incident, one she kept up and this time echoed by all The Kitchen. This was the one about the chamber-pots.

The chamber-pots were known as the Chambers, the Pots, the Vessels or the Yewties (UT's, short for utensils), and were placed under the beds at night at the same time that the mosquito nets were let down. The nets were vital for peaceful, mosquito-unmolested nights. Several yards of voluminous white netting were suspended above single beds by a circular hoop, the net itself held back during the day by wide satin ribbons decorated with a huge satin rosette or, in the case of my parents' four-poster, looped artistically up to the canopy. When let down at twilight they transformed familiar bedrooms into nightmare places. Unlit places where elongated white figures loomed limply on still nights … or, horror of horrors, billowed softly towards me in the breeze.…

As the youngest, I was the first to go up to bed. I did so on tiptoe so the Shapes wouldn't hear me, each creaking step reminding me of the story told (by Allan) of the little girl who was grabbed by one of those Shapes and Never Seen Again. An even more dreadful tale was about the little girl (it was never a little boy) whose leg was suddenly grabbed by a Thing which pulled her under the bed. They heard her screaming but when they looked under the bed where the screaming came from **there was no one there.**… When I crossed the upstairs landing and switched the lights on, the Shapes became mosquito nets once more and the Things lurking under the beds were clearly seen as chamber-pots, so I could get off my tiptoes and breathe again.

These chamber-pots were used because there was no electricity after nine o'clock and in the absence of street lighting the nights were blackest black. My own chamber-pot was small, of white enamel with a narrow black edge around the rim. My mother's was fuschia pink with a black handle, one of the set displayed on the wash-stand, consisting of a large china wash bowl and pitcher complete with matching toothbrush holders, sponge bowl, soap dish and slop pail, all splendidly decorated in fuschia, black and gold. The whole set was large and heavy and said to be very old. Breakage of any part of it, I often heard said, would be a real tragedy, and I had to remind myself of this whenever Woman Billy issued her threat. (Allan was always sent from the room when she did so, it not being the kind of thing for a growing boy to hear.)

When I grew to be a big girl, Woman Billy told me, I would have to **empty my mother's chamber pot.**

In The Kitchen they all nodded, serious-faced. This, they told me, was a daughterly duty, a mark of devotion. A rite of passage. Woman Billy, and every woman in The Kitchen it seemed, had emptied her mother's chamber-pot. My mother had no doubt emptied **her** mother's—and the time would come when I would have to do the same. When those mysterious hands that whisked the chamber-pot away in the morning no longer did so, then I would have to empty it. Not only that—I would have to clean it as well.

Woman Billy enjoyed describing the cleaning process. A piece of dried coconut husk was used to scrub the Pots out with a handful of sea-sand. They were then well rinsed. Next, Gossages brown soap was applied liberally, in and out, followed by another good rinse. The Pots were then dried and finally polished, inside and out, with a soft cloth. Dried coconut husk was to be replaced weekly, the cloths soaked in bleach before washing.

This threat was no doubt meant to be the Ultimate Deterrent, but in time there came Ultimate Deterrent II. When I was a big girl I would have to **empty the slop pails!** I almost believed this—until I tested my strength on the slop pail when no one was about and realized that not only was I tiny but I was built like a stick-insect, so this task would never be mine.

A good nanny, was how my mother described Woman Billy, always stressing that we were lucky to have found her. My mother would have preferred Old Simon to look after us, the nanny who had looked after Sister May and little Brother Jim, a truly legendary nanny who looked after babies of the staff ladies up and down the East Coast of Demerara and the West Coast. But Old Simon was old enough to be legendary whereas Woman Billy was young and besides, she Spoke Well. I was kept clean and safe against my will, and nothing was ever reported against her. Yes, the grown-ups agreed, we were lucky to have found her. I am not so sure Woman Billy was lucky to have found us or whether she even thought so herself. There cannot have been many nannies whose charges hurled cowdung at them.

Chapter Eleven

Pagli (she who mashed people and twisted their bones) lived in the coconut-thatch house which we passed on the way to visit our Grandmother. A trodden-earth yard surrounded it where a goat grazed, the boundaries marked by palings sprouting energetically with greenery, and barbed wire.

Pagli always seemed to be in the yard when we went by. A massive figure, bangled arms akimbo on massive hips, she watched us children with a keen eye. I scuttled by, feeling those arms grab me, feeling myself being mashed and twisted … and Woman Billy scuttled with me. Eager as she was to exchange how-de-do's with Pagli, she couldn't, I always took her by surprise, suddenly plunging both my hands into her pockets and pushing her forward with a force she never expected.

'Howdy Miz Pagli!' she would call over her shoulder as we rushed by. Pagli just looked at us and laughed, her single tooth showing.

I was sick with horror when I heard that she was coming to mash my mother.

'**And** twist your bones?'

'That too.' Mummy actually seemed pleased about it. 'The rainy weather does terrible things to bones. Wait till you're old, you'll see.'

I wondered if my mother knew what horrors would be performed on her or if indeed she knew the truth of Pagli's fearsome reputation. I wondered, too, at the deference shown by the Kitchen when Pagli appeared among them and the authority with which she swept through the house and heaved her huge bulk up the stairs to my mother's bedroom. Outside the half-opened door, I watched as she twisted her victim … left foot over right knee—right arm over both legs … grab the right ankle—breathe in—hold—breathe out—in—out—in—out—

Even more fascinating than the yogic contortions and the

sweet smelling hot-oil massage was the conversation that followed. Doors were always kept open upstairs to let the air circulate and keep the bedrooms cool, and I gave a good impression of being lost in my book if anyone checked on me. 'That child will damage her eyes' it was often said, 'Reading again.' So convinced were the adults of the authority their adulthood gave them, it never occurred to anyone that I had ears to hear and would actually listen when bidden not to. Especially when bidden not to … and so the conversations went on.…

Pagli's daughter, Beti, shy, subservient Beti, was suspected of Not Knowing Her Place. She was said to be giving the eye to one of the overseers Of all the overseers—Van Rjin!

He was known as Van Rjin and nothing else. Other overseers were Paddy, Jock, Scotty, Taffy or Mud'ead. No one ever addressed Van Rjin as Dutch. He was tall, blond, solitary and unsmiling. He was also startlingly good-looking. It was said that he was engaged to the daughter of an important Booker Man in England, a young lady expected to Inherit. No one knew if it was true or how the rumour started but it was said that Van Rjin was lost for love of her and had never looked at anyone else.

'So why that daughter of mine giving the man the eye, I don' know,' Pagli finished.

I wanted to run in and cry out that they were wrong, Beti never looked at him. It was he, Van Rjin whose head turned slowly (oh so slowly!) as she went by. Seated on his mule, he would even turn the animal so he could watch her retreating back. She was one of the Firewood Gang and carried an enormous basket of logs on her head, out-stuck arm paddling gently, hips swaying even more gently. Eyes down, head down, never a glance at the solitary figure on mule-back that watched, the watching figure whose every turn of the head seemed to plead silently with her to turn and look back at him. Perhaps if she had, none of it would ever have happened.

In the Kitchen they'd watched it happening, they knew all about it. The modest mien, the bent head, the refusal to meet Van Rjin's eye, all caused outcry and indignation. **Who** did that Beti think she was? Leading the poor man on like that! Him, of all people, so good-looking and engaged to a Booker Man's daughter too! Making her eye pass White-Man, that's what it was! Someone should talk to the girl, make her Know Her Place.

Pagli begged my mother to be that person. Otherwise there would be only one thing to do and Pagli would do it—give the girl a good beating. She wasn't too old—no daughter was too old to get a good beating from her mother. Especially a daughter who Didn't Know Her Place.

Beti was brought to the house one afternoon and taken to the room where my mother sat sewing. I was meant to be resting and The Kitchen was meant to be going about its business and not a whispered word came through the open door, so softly did they speak. My mother was at her most persuasive when she spoke softly. But word of Beti's stubborness got around anyway. And sure enough, the hips continued to sway, the dark head continued to be bowed, and Beti refused to raise her lovely head and look at Van Rjin.

It was a scandal, Aunt Vic declared, watching the performance from a kitchen window, the girl was **Bad**, she was just leading him on, the whole thing was a scandal from start to finish. It would all end badly.

The sounds of lamentation reached us one morning, distant wails that grew steadily louder and more sorrowful, and Pagli could be seen coming down the road, rending her long white hair in true Old Testament fashion. People getting water by the canal straightened up to watch, others ran to hear the dreadful news and fell in beside her, wailing too. Concerned friends rushed out of their houses to join them and small boys tagged along. They were a noisy procession by the time they reached our house.

Pagli collapsed at the foot of the back steps. She was a tragic figure, her face made shapeless by tears and grief, her long white hair in tatters around her head and her beseeching hands holding out great clumps of hair she had torn from a bleeding scalp. She and her followers implored my mother to DO SOMETHING!

Beti and Van Rjin had run off.

'They won't get far,' someone said, 'No farther than the stelling.' Heads nodded wisely. So it had happened. They would be stopped at the docks and brought back to face the music. Everyone looked forward to that, relishing the scene to come, the girl being given a good beating and made to Know Her Place. The man—!

But it seemed no one wanted them back.

Van Rjin was obviously untrustworthy, having gone native in this spectacular manner—and Beti! Beti would no longer be marriageable. Not for her the sumptuous wedding with the week-long festivities, not for her the transformation from barefoot wood-carrier to fairy princess. There was every possibility that Pagli would have torn her to shreds, the way she had torn her own hair.

The scandal remained fresh, the way scandal did in that small, self-contained world where the doings of fifty years past were as fresh as that day's. Word of Van Rjin drifted back from time to time. It was Big-People Business so I dared not ask, only listen with flapping ears. He had gone back to Holland where, it was said, he found a good job without any problem. He had, it appeared, Connections.

There were shrugs.

For Beti, there were not even shrugs. No one spoke of her. It was assumed that she had been abandoned somewhere Abroad once Van Rjin had 'used' her. That was all he'd wanted. What else did she expect? That he would **marry** her? The thought provoked laughter and not only among the white community, everyone had the same view on the affair. The girl couldn't be so stupid! Marriages like that were doomed. **Doomed.** Girls like Beti, barefoot girls from coconut-thatch houses, would not know how to go on Abroad. She would not know how to dress—how to cook European food—how to eat with a knife and fork—how to **behave**. All this had been pointed out to her, not only by my mother and hers but by everyone and their mother too. It did not seem to occur to anyone that Beti could learn. They agreed it was no one's fault but her own. The girl deserved all she got.

Someone back from home leave brought photographs from

England, an overseer who had been a friend of Van Rjin. They had met in London, he said, and he handed my mother the photographs without comment. She looked at them keenly for a long time, then put them down, also without comment.

I was older by then. I picked them up. The handsome figure of Van Rjin was unmistakable. Had I imagined that solitary air—? I must have done. He was smiling, he looked happy. Jovial, even. The woman beside him was smiling too, an elegant, dark-haired woman—Beti, no longer barefoot but high-heeled and fur-clad, with a gloss on her that many European women must have envied. And she wasn't looking decorously down at the ground before her, she was actually looking at Van Rijn. At last, she was looking at Van Rjin—actually, she was glowing at him.

Well. Everyone knew the Dutch were an odd race, they married people from strange parts of the world. Look at the way they had carried on when they ruled Guiana!

The Kitchen declared itself glad for the girl, and so did everyone else, but Pagli preferred to go on mourning.

Oddly enough, although girls were despised for not Knowing Their Place and aspiring to marry above their station, young men who did so were applauded and even encouraged. In their case, it was called Bettering Themselves. Most of the Bettering went on when they joined the Forces during the War and married English or European girls. There was a show of dismay among their parents but this was perfunctory and the pride with which they showed the photographs from abroad belied this. 'Look the girl hair! It yellow fo' true, eh!' 'Is bleach Ma, is bleach! They got good bleach in England.' The daughters of the family would run their fingers through their own luxuriant tresses, their blacker-than-midnight tresses, with little smiles.

The young man's sisters were quick to see the marriage as a gateway to a wider world for themselves, and so it frequently turned out to be. The parents of any girl he had been 'sweet' on were usually more relieved than dismayed, for no one knew how long the War would last and it took only a few short years for a marriageable daughter to become unmarriageable. Dowries were not the problem that they were in India, girls were keen to marry and unwilling to wait for someone who might even decide not to return.

So after the initial complaints about letting the family down ('not even a proper wedding!') there would be a helpless shrugging of shoulders and talk about young people nowadays doing what they liked, with no consideration for the old folk. There seemed to be a general acceptance that times were changing and that sons who went abroad would not return the same sons who had left.

Some of the men may well have taken their war brides back to Guiana when travelling became easier. I did hear of a war widow who took her small fair-haired son to visit his grandparents at at Enmore. He was admired and wept over and both parties were excessively nice to each other. The little boy and his mother took the next ship back to England. What they thought of the range-dwelling and the sugar plantation is not known.

That was felt to be the end of the story, the parties had, after all, nothing in common only her dead husband. The expression 'culture shock' was not yet in use but it was implied.

But it was not the end. At her invitation, his sisters soon left to join her in England, and were reported to be doing well. They had both got into college without any problem, having been educated and chastised at Enmore school.

Our Grandmother ('Mother') could always be spotted on the road when she was coming to see us. She was short and plump with silver-white hair and wore dark, ankle-length dresses and a wide-brimmed brown hat. It was not this that made her easy to spot, it was the retinue that always accompanied her.

It *was* a retinue. People just seemed to appear on that empty road: they would all stop and chat … and shortly they would be joined by more people. The original chatters would fall behind, Mother would take a few steps forward and then there would be a pause for the recent joiners to take up the conversation … and so it went on. The leaving-taking before she came to our house was almost ceremonial. The attitude of the retinue was deferential.

Why? I wondered. It seemed in some way remarkable.

'Why are those old people always with Mother?' I would ask. 'All of them rushing to speak to her when they see her and walking and talking? They are always doing it! What have they got to talk about?'

My mother would say shortly, 'They knew her when she was a child.'

'More likely they think she's the Queen of England.' Aunt Vic was always sarcastic about Mother's retinue.

It was all a puzzle to me. Also puzzling was why, on our afternoon walks, Woman Billy and I were so often stopped by groups of very old people who seemed to want only to look at me. I was skinny and round-faced with straight fly-away hair and was often told I was an unattractive child—'Not good-looking like your brother' (Aunt Vic.) But I was made to stop while the oldies looked at me and uttered admiring sounds. 'Is Miz Stokes' grandchile,' they would nod to each other, murmuring.

Miz Stokes' grandchild—? I knew nothing about Miz Stokes. I had always thought I was Mother's grandchild.

Both Woman Billy and The Kitchen kept their mouths firmly shut when questioned about Miz Stokes and her grandchild. I knew all the signs: this was Big-People Business. So I asked my mother about Miz Stokes. I had realised by then that there were many many things never spoken of simply because They Must Never Be Spoken Of. But this I had to know.

'Where did you hear that name?' I was asked. Almost angrily, I thought.

Why my mother should have been angry, I do not know; she must always have known it was inevitable that, living at Enmore, at some time or other I would hear the name of Stokes. Perhaps it just took her by surprise.

I told her about the very old people who sometimes stopped Woman Billy and me. Just to look at me.

The answer came back as before. 'They knew Mother when she was a child.' Then, after consideration, 'Mother's maiden name, the name she had before she was married, was Stokes. She was Miss Stokes.'

'You mean her father was called Mr. Stokes?'

'Yes.' The answer was short and not encouraging.

'And so her mother was Mrs. Stokes?'

There was no answer. I was well aware of what sudden icy silences meant. This one forbade me to pursue the topic.

I did not pursue it but I did not let it go away. I heard the muttering in The Kitchen and I became more and more curious.

'Is time somebody tell the chile. She growing.'

'Tell she? Somebody like who? Like you? Not me!'

But I knew I had only to wait, to listen. The Kitchen gossiped all day except when my mother was present. The white-haired ex-Kitchen inhabitants who sometimes tottered up the back steps 'to see how the Mistress an' al'you doin', they gossiped too. They had worked in other kitchens besides ours and they had a lot to say. Given large tinnin mugs of highly-sugared tea and chunks of cake (or slices of bread and butter with thick brown sugar in the absence of cake) they gossiped at length— but again, never when Aunt Vic was in residence. She would announce to my mother in her sewing-room that 'the alms house was open again.'

My mother's reply was always a satisfied nod and a smile. These were regular callers, the people who would have been her Old Retainers had not Aunt Vic been in the habit of turning up and taking over and driving them out.

'I'll give them time to finish their tea, then I'll go down and see them.' she would say.

It happened very differently.

One day I noticed some pictures on the wall at Mother's house. They had probably always been there but I hadn't been tall enough to see them in any detail. Now, I saw a group of ladies in long dresses, old-fashioned dresses, sitting on wicker chairs and gentlemen with large moustaches standing behind them. They were posed in front of what was clearly the Enmore

Manager's House. (The Managers' Houses, at that time, were simply known as that, the Manager's House or Manja House. Recent books, mostly fiction, about Guiana now refer to these most impressive buildings as 'The Great House.' I never heard them called that when I was growing up there, nor did any of my friends who grew up on the sugar plantations in Guiana. 'The Great House' was a term found only in books about the Deep South.)

'Who are those people?' I asked.

'People—?'

'In funny clothes.'

'Funny—? Ah. That was the management staff and their wives. Those pictures were taken a long time ago when Mr. Stokes, the new Manager at Enmore took over. He took over from his brother, another Mr. Stokes. They were both Managers there.'

I ventured carefully. 'Mr Stokes? You mean … your Daddy?'

She said without pause, 'That's right. Look, there they are, standing side by side, behind their wives, Young Mrs. Stokes and Younger Mrs. Stokes.'

Oh! Young Mrs. Stokes and Younger Mrs.—two Mrs. Stokes! 'Why were they called that?'

'I expect one was young and the other was younger.'

I nodded. That sounded reasonable. Then, daringly, 'Which one was your Mummy?'

My grandmother seemed prepared for this question.

'Neither of them. I was what is known as an Outside Child.'

I was too young, too sheltered, to know what that meant. I had never heard the expression Outside Child before. I must have looked bewildered.

'Mr. Stokes, the plantation Manager, was my father. My mother, your great-grandmother, was not his wife. I was born outside the marriage. She, my mother, was an indentured East Indian girl who worked in the Manager's House. The previous Manager, the previous Mr. Stokes. I think she may have helped in the nursery.'

Had I been older—**had I been older!**—I would have asked

the questions I still need to ask. But I couldn't form the words. I could only look at my grandmother, silenced by this sudden revelation, questions half-formed whirling around in my head.

'That sort of thing happened a lot in those days.' A kind hand was laid on my head. 'When you are older you will understand.'

I am older, but the questions are still there.

Did the indentured Indian girl come to Guiana all by herself? Did she come with her parents and siblings?

Or were mother and daughter running away from a tyrannical father, a wife-beating husband? One heard of many cases like that. The agents in India who recruited employees for the sugar plantations were paid a higher price for women than for men, so they asked no questions.

How old had she been? Were there any photographs? (I saw none.)

When Mr. Stokes returned to live in England with his wife and family, when he left Guiana and returned to live there forever as most English plantation managers did, did he leave the Indian girl and her child behind? **His** child?

Well, of course he did. Silly question.

What was her name?

Did the Young (or the Younger) Mrs. Stokes know about her?

Perhaps she did. Both Mrs. Stokes were local girls, I learned later. This was not unusual in those days, the days when many of the plantations were privately owned. Later, the Firm who bought them out preferred their English employees, their management staff and overseers to marry English wives. The father of one of the Mrs. Stokes was an Englishman, a well-established businessman in Georgetown. They were a wealthy family.

Mrs. Stokes would have taken her immediate servitors with her when she married and went to her new home at Enmore. The old family nanny would have been brought out of retirement, as old family nannies frequently were, to look after the inevitable new baby. The laundry maid who looked after Mrs. Stokes's clothes, who did all the hand-washing and the ironing, that most valuable person could not possibly have been left behind. There would have been a manservant or two, very likely even a butler. A newly-married young woman from a wealthy background, a Guianese young woman, would not have moved into the Manager's House at Enmore without a backbone of her own staff. Her parents would have seen to that, it would all have been arranged for her.

But—had Mrs. Stokes known about the Outside baby? Or had it been kept from her in the same way that things were kept from me? That would not have been difficult. A job in the Manja's House was a job to be valued, smart uniforms were supplied, the accommodation was a cut above the normal range dwelling, many perks came with that job. Many perks. And, of course, there was the status. If keeping your mouth shut about a situation that was, after all, common in the colony at that time (and obviously even in the Manja's House) was what you had to do to keep that position, then you did it. You kept your mouth shut.

But—had Mr. Stokes put all his cards on the table when asking for her hand in marriage? Or was illegitimacy so common in the Colony that everyone knew about it, and it was simply accepted as normal? Would the Young Mrs. Stokes (or the Younger Mrs. Stokes) have known all about it the Outside Child, did she feel it was just the way things were, and she would not have allowed it in any way to impinge on her position as the Manager's wife?

I was never to know. It was not discussed. None of this ever occurred to me until years later.

There was something else I was never to know and I go over the scene time and again, trying to recall the conversation, knowing that in my youth and my ignorance, my overwhelming bewilderment, I had missed something.

Something important.

I go over and over that conversation on that faraway day in a faraway land, with a grandmother long gone.

'You mean ... your Daddy?'

'Yes,' Mother said, 'There were two brothers, Alfred and Harry Stokes. Both were Managers at Enmore, one took over from his brother. Look, there they are, the two brothers, side by side, *standing in the row behind their wives.'*

Of course. Their wives. Young Mrs. Stokes and Younger Mrs. Stokes.

But my grandmother never indicated which Mr. Stokes she meant. She did not raise a hand, nor did she lift a finger to indicate. She did not speak his name.

No, she did not.

So ... was it Alfred or was it Harry?

Why did I not ask?

Alfred and his family left Guiana when he retired and settled in Devon, where the Stokes family originally came from. Harry's family also settled in Devon. But Harry, I am told, did not leave Guiana. He died there and was buried at Enmore. My grandmother's grave is not far from his. But where is the grave of the indentured girl who bore my grandmother? No one has anything to tell me. I have a forlorn hope that she is perhaps in Enmore churchyard too.

I do know that my grandmother was called Mary Ann Stokes.

So was the mother of Alfred and Harry.

But I still do not know which of her sons was my great-grandfather.

Chapter Twelve

The travelling trunks stood in those dark recesses of the dressing-room where Woman Billy always told me the hairy black spiders lived. The trunks had been in that spot for so long they had become invisible to me, I saw them only when reminded. 'You don't want to wear your vest—! Wait till I tell those spiders!' Or 'You kick off your shoes! One of these days—you hear me?—one of these days they will move the trunks and **then**—!

But the Day of the Arachnids never came. One day the trunks were indeed heaved out and polished up and the space they left was revealed to be just an empty space. Surprisingly, not a single spider. The threat that had hung over me was forgotten in the excitement of that day and the days that followed.

This was what trunks were for! This rushing back and forth that adults did, their arms full of neatly folded clothes ... toiletries, sticking plaster and Dettol, all to be checked off on lists.... I had always wondered what lay inside the dull blue exteriors of those trunks. Polished up they were shiny again, the brass trimmings glowed and I could see my face in them. One was simply an empty trunk but the other, standing on its end, actually had drawers and hanging wardrobe space. I was allowed to stick on the labels that said WANTED ON VOYAGE.

We were going to Barbados!

'I've got a ripley bathing-suit,' Biddy told me—the Fitz-Geralds were also going—and I longed for a ripley bathing-suit just like Biddy's.

'Of course, dear,' my mother said absently, busy with her lists. I examined them hourly to see if the ripley bathing-suit had been added but the lists seemed to contain mostly bed linen, table linen, cutlery, china and towels. We were renting a bungalow on the St. Lawrence beach and had to take all the household equipment for a six-month stay. That included Aunt Vic's favourite pots and pans as she refused to use any supplied with the bungalow—'other people's rubbish!'

It must have been a giant feat of organisation for my mother, who usually needed days to plan a trip to Georgetown. I later learned that she had kept the lists from the previous stay in Barbados, years earlier, complete with notes she had made on them. This was felt to be doubly useful as we were returning to the same bungalow we'd rented before. Besides the trunks and suitcases, huge wicker chests were produced, to be lined with old sheets, packed and re-packed several times and labelled NOT WANTED ON VOYAGE.

The *Lady Hawkins*, one of the fleet of Canadian steamships known as the Lady Boats, was to take us to Barbados. Not only was Aunt Vic going with us—to supervise the housekeeping she made it known, convinced as always that no one else was capable of doing so—but also going with us was Sybil, a young relative of my mother's (a step-sister of my mother's family, I think, though this was never confirmed to me) whose vague responsibility it was to look after us children. I was hugely relieved to hear that Woman Billy was being left behind.

It seemed that everyone who had ever worked in The Kitchen, as well as general well-wishers, came up the back steps during the days before we left to talk about the coming journey and wish us a safe return. 'Girls' who had been driven from the door in tears by Aunt Vic returned smiling and bearing no ill-will, Yard Grannies reluctantly dismissed for being found sleeping too deeply too often came, wide-awake. Batches of biscuits had been made and these, with tinnin mugs of hot sugared tea, everyone enjoyed as they gossiped, laughed, reminisced and exclaimed on how we children had grown. When the biscuits ran out the latecomers were given bread dripping with condensed milk which they seemed to enjoy just as much. When the condensed milk ran out the stragglers were offered buttered bread sprinkled with brown sugar. I looked longingly at all these treats but Woman Billy said they were bad for my teeth.

There was great emphasis on wishing us a safe journey there and back. They would pray for us, everyone stressed, God, or Allah, be with us always some beseeched, falling to their knees on the spot, hands clasped in prayer and pointing heavenwards. My mother thanked them and with some prodding we children did so too. For not only were we going on what seemed like a long and unaccustomed journey at that time, but the year was 1939. Talk of war and the fear of war had reached even Guiana.

Miss Dorothea Jackson and Miss Florence McKinnon said a different goodbye, for they were leaving my life. When we returned in September I would be going to boarding-school, to the Ursuline Convent in Georgetown. Miss Jackson hoped albeit doubtfully that I would make progress with my arithmetic, while Miss McKinnon was convinced I would be successful in all that I did as I 'had a good ear,' she told my mother but she did not mean for music as I thought. 'A very good listener,' she elaborated. Both teachers wished me well formally and I thanked them just as formally for all they had done for me. We all shook hands. Miss Jackson would never arrive on her sit-up-and-beg bicycle again nor Miss McKinnon tell her tales Under-The-House. They must have missed her there as much as I did.

The English members of the staff were openly envious. Not for us the long voyages back to the UK and disembarkation at places like Liverpool or Greenock (the very names provoked groans). My father had saved up his long leaves (three months was usually allowed) so we had six months of holiday ahead of us beginning with the voyage through the Caribbean islands before we reached Barbados. 'I'd like to do that too,' the UK-bound would say longingly, 'But the wife, y' know.... Her family ... all back home ... wouldn't hear of it.'

Trinidad was our first stop, the nearest island to the South American mainland. Once part of the mainland, it had broken off sometime in pre-history. A wealthy island because of its pitch lake, a lush green island with something I'd seen only in books—MOUNTAINS! Rivers were there and streams and greenery to feast our scenery-starved eyes on. It was my first remembered sight of scenery which, until then, had been something that hung in pictures on walls, something seen in books and far removed from the brown, dried-up flatlands of the East Coast, Demerara. And there were cool cool breezes.

I wanted to stay there forever.

I also wanted to stay forever in Grenada. Miss McKinnon had told me that it was called the Spice Island and she said we would smell the cinnamon and nutmeg before we landed. I don't remember if we did. What I remember is the winding road that climbed up green mountains and the dark lake that was said to be bottomless. A bottomless lake....That meant, Allan was eager to explain, that if I fell in I would sink forever. Just go on sinking, sinking, forever and ever, into eternity.... Another remembered sight was the red tiled roofs of the capital, St. George's, where I first heard about tiles being shaped on the naked thighs of dusky maidens.

The next eye-widening wonder, the quite unforgettable wonder, was the diving boys. Further into the Caribbean Sea, the water became clear turquoise and at every anchorage little boats with small boys skimmed over the water toward the ship, their skinny bodies and pleading faces revealing none of the expertise that would soon be on show. They looked eager and hungry, holding up their hands to the passengers looking down from the deck rail ... until the coins spun—up—up into the air and down ... and the brown bodies leapt and shot into the water and hands closed around the pennies and sixpences before their descent had barely begun.

Those were the hungry ones. The others—the show-offs, the experienced ones with their eyes on bigger prizes—waited until the novelty wore off then began their spectacular dives from one side of the ship, under the keel to the other side—surfacing with wide grins and barely a gasp for air. Long after the passengers had stopped holding their breath, they bobbed up with a huge didn't-think-I-could-do-it-did-you grin. The onlookers dug into their pockets for even bigger coins and sometimes wrapped notes around them to throw down into the boats, now conveniently hauled closer. These coins—and notes!—were retrieved before our eyes. I don't think a single one was ever lost.

After that performance (it took several hours) they rowed or swam away waving and calling and we all stood at the deck-rail and waved back. 'Sea urchins' one passenger called them.

They were a unique experience, never before seen or even imagined by two small children from Enmore.

The months in Barbados were full of kindly sun and cool breezes, long leisurely hours for our parents, picnic hampers to be prepared, whole days spent in green and lovely places, winding drives through cane-fields, friendly, smiling people. And something I had never known until then. Nothing in my few years had prepared me for what I was given in Barbados.

Freedom!

Freedom to walk barefooted on a deserted beach with only Biddy or Allan and Desmond for company. To dash in and out of the water, thought shallow and safe behind the coral reef, sometimes barely covering our feet. To leave my hat under a rock and never wear it. To go back to the bungalow only when driven to do so by thirst or hunger. To spend my days without the following shadow of a nanny.

Freedom from Woman Billy!

Decades later, recalling those times, I told my mother how good that first freedom had felt. How savoured … how never forgotten. And my mother, who had lost two children to the tropics and who had lived throughout our childhood (and beyond!) with the ever-present threat of malaria, yellow fever, typhoid, scorpions, snakes and many nameless dreads of which I was but dimly aware, said only, 'It was good to be able to give you that freedom.'

There was so much to see, so many tales to hear, happy ones and unusual ones, sometimes downright dreadful ones. Tales that would have been deemed unsuitable for us to hear in Guiana were discussed openly. Never forgotten by those who heard it, was the story of the Chase Vault in the Christ Church Cemetery.

The vault had been built in the previous century for members of the Chase family and their friends. However loving and friendly they may have been when alive, their remains became distinctly unfriendly when interred. Whenever the vault was opened to receive another occupant, the coffins were found to be **in violent disarray**. This caused so much talk among the population that the Chase funerals became very much larger than the average funeral, as people gathered from all over the island to see for themselves.

There was no explanation. No mini-earthquakes that could have thrown the coffins about, no evidence of break-ins by ill-wishers, no reason at all. Except for one....

The Chase family were known throughout the Caribbean to be particularly cruel—horrendously so—to their slaves. During his lifetime Mr. Chase was said to be the most hated man on the island. The cruelty and torture he meted out was unspeakable: strong men rushed away and vomited when they heard about it. There was only one conclusion.

The spirits of the slaves would not let them rest.

A Governor new to the island decided that he would put an end to it. It had gone on long enough. The vault was opened, the coffins re-arranged in the order in which they had originally been laid and the floor spread with sand which would show footsteps. The simple explanation that human hands were responsible for the skulduggery would be clear to all. The door of the vault was sealed with the Governor's personal seal. Native superstition would finally be put to rest.

But native superstition refused to rest.

When the Governor's seal was broken and the vault opened, the coffins were found to be in even more disarray. There were no footsteps on the sand. The Governor decided that there was only one thing to do: he ordered that the coffins be removed from the vault and each one buried separately in different parts of the island. They have remained where put, alone and immobile. The Chase Vault is now empty.

The story of the Vault is famous in Barbados; a visit to the Vault is a must on the tourists' itinerary, and the locals love re-telling the tale.

Before the end of our holiday, we left the bungalow in St. Lawrence to stay in Half Moon Fort. This was an old military fort in St. Lucy, in the north of the island, a place my parents knew well, they had stayed there before and were overjoyed at the thought of returning. Daddy was a Mason and one night he returned from a Lodge meeting with the happy news that he had met the owner and arranged to rent the Fort for the rest of our holiday. What joy! It was as though we had won the Lottery! Half Moon Fort was a delightful place built on rocks looking out to a crashing sea, a place which gave every impression of being steeped in history. I felt sure there would be many, many tales to hear.

If there were—there must have been!—I don't remember them. Something I saw in St. Lucy blew all thought of disturbed coffins and cemeteries out of my mind.

We were driving among the cane fields when my mother's voice grew suddenly agitated, high-pitched, adding to the unreality of that sight. '*PAM! Don't stare! Turn away! Don't be so rude! Close your mouth—don't gawp! Stop staring—STOP—*' Then: 'Driver—get us away from here! Quickly!' The car speeded up but I turned my head and went on gawping. I didn't know what I was looking at, it made no sense to me. My squeaking protestations went on non-stop all the way back to the Fort. *We should have stopped and picked him up! We should have given him a good long shower! Didn't you see how dirty he was, Mummy? We should have given him a proper meal, you saw how thin he was, we should have found him some decent clothes, he was in rags—rags! Surely you saw—! Mummy, how could you leave him there!*

What I had seen was a boy sitting on the edge of a cane-field. Long arms, long bare legs, all bone thin, a battered soft felt hat. Bare, filthy feet. A teenager … he looked as though he had been working in the fields. But he couldn't possibly—! How could he! He was covered in rags and had a piece of red rag beside him—I remember the brightness of it, the redness of it—and he seemed to be eating his lunch out of it. A very ordinary sight, a sight one saw among the cane-fields every day in Barbados. Black boys sitting by cane-fields just having their lunch. Nothing unusual about it.

But there was.

This boy was white.

His hair under the soft felt hat was blond and his eyes which looked at me all the while I gawped at him, were very very blue. He was white indeed. White-white. Almost transparent.

It was the first time I ever saw a Po'White.

We simply drove on.

The original slaves in Barbados were white. Their history seems to have become lost, ignored, bypassed, neglected, only recently have academics begun to research it and write about it. There are some who say it is all a myth, it never happened. Not so. The history is alive in Barbados and the descendants of the white slaves are there, many of them still on the plantations their forebears were assigned to all those centuries ago. The white slaves preceded the Africans and were sent to the colony by the shipload in the 1600s. Oliver Cromwell scooped them up, the Irish, destitute and rebellious after the Famine; the landless, displaced Scots who did not to go to America; the vagrants, itinerants, the jobless, the hopeless and the mentally retarded in England, they were were herded together by Cromwell's men and transported to the Caribbean, mainly to Barbados. Most of them would not have stood a chance of leading good lives in their own countries, let alone in the tropical heat, where they were badly housed and poorly fed.

No firsthand record survives of their journey, few if any of them would have been able to read or write. The arrival of the ships that bore them to Barbados was unlike that of the slave ships from Africa, for those transported on the latter were inventoried on leaving Africa and purchased when they arrived. They represented money. The ships that brought the black gold mattered more than the ones which offered up the white dregs of the British population; the arrival of the slave ships were recorded and their cargo once more checked, the losses listed, the purchase and destination of the slaves also recorded.

They were said to be indentured, that first shipment of the hopeless. Maybe they were. The legal documents, the Indentures, appeared to have been devised for the sole purpose of being lost by those indentured. Each document was written out in duplicate on a single sheet of paper: the paper was then cut in half by a serrated knife and one half given to the master, the other to the indentured. When the time of the contract expired, usually five or seven years, the two pieces of paper were put together and if they matched up that proved them to be genuine and they were honoured.

It is unlikely that many of the transported realised the value of those pieces of paper. Maybe their papers were lost, disintegrated, used to light fires ... at any rate few of them were honoured. The unfortunates laboured in the cane-fields as best they could, and most simply took root on parishes in the far north of the island, where they were originally left. Many of their descendants have been there ever since. The conditions in which they lived and still live led to them being called 'Poor Whites'.

Thereafter the other shiploads of white immigrants were more fortunate. The planters requested a superior type of person, the kind who could make themselves useful as domestic servants, cooks familiar with English-style food, laundresses who could iron the intricate styles worn and teach the female slaves how to do so, as well as butlers and footmen to add class to the planters' residences, now becoming very grand indeed. These people were given indentures which were honoured when the time came. The descendants of the more fortunate ones went on to lead good lives, to become prominent businessmen in the Caribbean, while some became famous sportsmen.

We returned to Guiana in September; war had been declared on the day before my birthday. In the hours before the dawn, my mother sat by her bedroom window and wept. I could hear Daddy trying to console her, urging her to look forward to the next holiday.

'In only three years we will be there again, think of that.'

But she wept even more. 'The children are growing,' she cried, 'And who knows how long this war will last! That was our last holiday as a family, I know it James, I know it!'

She was right. It was our last holiday together.

I fell asleep to the sound of her sorrow.

Woman Billy re-appeared the next morning and bore us off to our Grandmother's house. There was all that unpacking to be done at home, the trunks to be heaved back into position in the dressing-room, and the children to be kept out of the way. The Kitchen was re-activated and Joseph came to light the stove. Aunt Vic was once more in charge.

In Mother's house, I saw with new eyes the Alma-Tadema style prints and wall-hangings … impossibly romantic scenes of beautiful women and beseeching lovers, all under a sky of unbelievable blue against a background of turquoise sea.

'It was like exactly like **that**,' I said firmly when asked about our holiday, and everyone laughed.

The Convent loomed. I thought it was the largest building I had ever seen but my mother said not so, it just seemed large, the factory at Enmore was a lot larger but familiarity had made it seem small. I gazed up and on at the huge white edifice and tried to believe her. But not only were the Convent buildings large and spread out, they appeared to cover a large part of the block and there were **walls.**

Walls!

'It look like a prison, eh,' Ramnarine, the driver, muttered under his breath but my mother heard and rebuked him with that slight stiffening of her shoulders she was so good at. He slunk back to the car and we were admitted to what I had already begun to think of as the Convent portals.

The Portuguese who originally went to Guiana as indentured labour did not labour for long. They were from Madeira, then a poor island, and unsuited to the equatorial heat. They left the land as soon as they could and started small businesses, mainly in Georgetown. As they prospered, they felt the need for a good Roman Catholic school for their daughters. Portugal was a Roman Catholic country, and Catholics took their religion with them wherever they went. So they invited the Ursuline nuns to come to Guiana to start a school. The Irish nuns were sent by the Vatican and the result was St. Rose's High School, where the daughters of Portuguese, East Indian, African, Dutch, French, English and other races mixed happily and received a superior education. Not only Roman Catholic girls but also Protestants, Jews, Hindus, and Muslims mixed with the daughters of confirmed atheists.

They, and their descendants, we Ursuline Convent girls, learned the meaning of the word 'integration' long before the rest of the world started using it.

Miss Murphy, who let us through the portals on that initial visit, was the doorkeeper/receptionist. A tiny, white-haired cottage-loaf lady, always in a white, long-sleeved blouse and long black skirt, she had seen many little girls come and go. My cousin Biddy was one of those she had seen go. Aged five and placed in the Montessori, Biddy decided by mid-morning on her first day that now she had been to school, she didn't like it and would go home. She left the bright little classroom and the chair with her name on it, walked boldly through the door and set off for home with an astonished Miss Murphy in pursuit. A man on a bicycle finally caught up with her.

Reverend Mother Angela Woods wore the title of Reverend Mother with awesome dignity, the first nun I had ever seen. Tall and kindly, she was expert at putting mothers and would-be pupils at ease. That first interview with her was the only one, from then on Dormitory Mistresses, Form Mistresses, Games Mistresses, and other kinds of Mistresses took over.

Mother Magdalen, the Dormitory Mistress, was energetic, lively, brilliantly blue-eyed, and beautiful to look at, even in the enveloping black-and-white habit that was meant to obliterate the wearer's looks and personality. Trinidadian-born, her family had a plantation on that island and she had the great advantage over nuns transplanted from abroad of being used to the climate and customs and being familiar with the West Indian mind and language. She gave us a tour of parts of the Convent that would be relevant to my life there 'so you can always picture Pam here,' she told my mother, who said later that she was able to do just that and found it comforting.

We were shown the classrooms where I would sit, the Assembly Hall with its magnificent floor and even more magnificent stage where I was one day to be a Violet at Dawn, Beth in 'Little Women' and Elizabeth Bennet in 'Pride and Prejudice'. The dormitory ... the salle (à manger) where day pupils had their meals and the place where Katy, the sweetie-lady brought her basket and sold her confectionery on weekdays ... my mother was impressed, even more impressed when other nuns passed by and nodded, smiling at us. We, or certainly I, imagined that all nuns would be like that.

I had been there a few years when the American nuns arrived with great fanfare. They clearly thought they had Much Work to Do in our backward little Colony and seemed surprised to find us well-mannered, well-behaved and well on the way to becoming well-educated. But—they did what the English nuns had not done, they showed us a gateway out of Guiana to the rest of the world. To us, England had always been a faraway place we might someday see. Arrival of the American nuns brought the outside world, mainly North America closer—and desirable. We no longer sang *Early One Morning* and songs that ended with Hey Nonny No; *Old Black Joe* and *Swanee River* entered our repertoire.

History, too, came alive. The American War of Independence seemed to have ended only a few years previously and became more real to us than the war still going on in Europe. Longfellow took over from Tennyson, Hiawatha hunted among the pine trees by the shores of Gitchee Gumee and the American nuns prepared us for the world outside Guiana.

But with their coming, strange new words seeped into our vocabulary. Words like intolerance—prejudice—colour consciousness—oppression. I couldn't wait to take these new words home, to tell my parents the many wrongdoings our masters in England and we in the Colony had been guilty of all these years—especially, it seemed, we who lived on the sugar plantations.

Slavery! We had heard the word all our lives but never knew what wickedness it represented. The wickedness of our forefathers, those first colonists and the abominable way they had treated the slaves....

I saw the looks my parents exchanged over my head and knew that they would take this talk of slavery and oppression and all these new words no further. So I dashed into The Kitchen later, still intent on pursuing the subject. Surely **they** would want to talk about it? To hear of these new feelings of guilt, of remorse and compassion that tore me, now that my eyes had been opened? To talk about how **they** felt after these years of being ground into submission—not only they but their parents! Their parents' parents! Who knew how much farther back! How **they** felt after all this time of this unjust, this cruel, unforgivable oppression....

'What you want, Missy?'

Absolution! That was what I wanted from them—absolution!

But in The Kitchen I was sharply dismissed. 'Look chile—if you got nothing better to do, go do it somewhere else—don' humBUG a'we!'

Sometimes they said, 'Chile, is tiresome you tiresome! Why you don' ask Annie or Susan these same questions you ask a'we?'

'A'we' in The Kitchen were all the descendants of the African slaves. Annie and Susan were Water Carriers, the girls who brought large containers of water to The Kitchen in dry weather. They were also Log Carriers and brought wide baskets of red logs which they delivered daily to the staff kitchens, the huge baskets balanced miraculously on their heads.

They were East Indians. Their forebears were the indentured labourers who had taken the place of the freed African slaves. They also had crossed the sea in ships but, unlike the slaves, they were not shackled. They were, in theory, free, and went to Guiana to work under contract for an agreed time and a free voyage back to India was written into their contract.

The agents who contracted them naturally painted Guiana as The Promised Land. Life and work there would be easy, rewarding, there would be opportunities for advancement, even becoming their own masters. Those who signed on expected to be able to send for their families, or even to return with riches.

Most stayed.

Indentured labour was the brainchild of Sir John Gladstone (father of the future Prime Minister William Gladstone) who owned sugar plantations in Guiana. Portuguese and Chinese labour was used initially, but not for long. Used to a different climate, they were defeated by the Guianese sun and dropped like flies. The East Indians came from Uttar Pradesh (hence East Indians) and were used to labouring in the equatorial heat.

They did the work of the slaves. They were fed as the slaves had been fed. They were housed in the same one-room dwellings as the slaves. They were treated like slaves. They were even called slaves.

I can remember hearing them referred to as 'indentured slaves'. The plantocracy, having always been surrounded by slaves, had 'slavery' stamped throughout their psyche.

Even as a small child I was aware that socializing with the workers' children, even any exchange of words, was a strict NO-NO. So I never spoke to Annie or Susan, apart from a quiet 'Good morning' and a shy smile, always returned just as quietly and shyly. To be truthful, I may not have spoken to them even if encouraged. I realise now that it was their appearance that silenced me and kept me thoroughly overwhelmed. East Indian girls were almost invariably beautiful, breathtakingly so, and I thought Annie and Susan, clad in serviceable old clothes, barefooted, dusty, faces bare of any enhancement, were the most beautiful of them all.

But I longed for conversation with girls of my age. Not with the few visiting staff children from other plantations, whose lives were so similar to mine, but with the children of the workers. How many brothers and sisters did they have? What did they do in school? What did they eat, did they really have curry-and-roti every day? We had curry only when my parents had informal lunch parties, or best of all, when the meat sent from The Meat Company in Georgetown had not survived the journey and was 'off'. Then we had only ground provisions and a curry sauce worked magic with these. It was especially magical with boring English Potatoes.

So I had no longed-for chats with the children on the plantation and I did not know how they lived. I had never seen a range-dwelling until I saw Cookie's, so I knew nothing about them. I was amazed to learn that quite large families actually lived in one room, and not a particularly large room at that.

It was mainly the fact that sometimes three generations

lived in that one room that ruled out socializing. Little girls who lived in one room with all their family knew and saw things little girls should not know and see. Not only about life and death but about conception and birth. They would have seen their grandparents die, sometimes peacefully, sometimes not. They would have seen and heard their younger siblings being conceived and seen them being born. (This latter fact was felt to be particularly scandalous by the staff wives.)

They also knew about knife cuttings and nose bobs—those punishments inflicted for infidelity, suspected, reported or real, the bobs usually made with a sharp cutlass.

Some of them knew about murder.

'These are things little girls like you should not know about,' Woman Billy told me sternly.

'What about little boys?' I asked.

My brother, Allan, sometimes played cricket with a select group of the workers' sons.

'It don't matter about little boys.' She shrugged. 'Now, don't let your Mummy know you hear that in The Kitchen!' A finger wagged at me. 'If she know, the whole Kitchen get sack! Mebbe me fust…' she finished thoughtfully.

Chapter Thirteen

My Uncle John FitzGerald had what we children thought was the most marvellous job in the world and the most enviable. We were not the only ones who thought so: successful businessmen who visited his domain audibly wondered where they had gone wrong and what they were doing with their lives. Uncle John used to say that he was responsible for an area larger than Barbados but without the population. That area was the East Demerara Water Conservancy, better known as the Lamaha. He supervised a catchment area of 260 square miles where rivers were damned for irrigating the sugar plantations and the coastal villages. It also supplied Georgetown with water for industrial uses, though not for drinking. Huge wooden vats in the back-yards collected water in the rainy season and provided for that need. My uncle did this vital job with one assistant and a small staff, travelling the rivers, the creeks and the savannahs in a launch, sometimes taking visitors with him.

I had always known about Lama, as his headquarters was called, I had grown up hearing about the place, Biddy and my FitzGerald cousins talked of it so much and I had been promised so many times that I could go there 'one day' that I had simply stopped thinking about it. So it came as a surprise to me: I had not imagined that scenery like that could be found in Guiana. It was beyond dreaming. The damming of the rivers flooded the savannahs and created a wetlands wonderland of blooms and waterfowl that was magic to see and hear.

We made our way through the savannahs in a corial (a dug-out, a boat carved by the Indians (the Aborigine Indians) from the trunk of a tree). It was manned by one of the Indians, the water barely centimetres away from the gunwale, voices hushed and paddles quiet. Not far away, we all knew, under those lilies and water hyacinths where long-legged birds picked their way elegantly, alligators, caiman and water monsters lurked—more afraid of us, Uncle Johnny kept stressing, than we were of them. We tried to believe him.

The headquarters of the Conservancy where the staff lived was a small settlement on the banks of the dark, deep Lamaha River. There were workshops, a few employees' houses, boathouses, a guest house and of course the Manager's house which was The Old House, the original building, and the New House, a much larger large rambling wooden building with no outside walls. It was wide open to the wind and the stunning views, which we children loved. The roofs of both houses, and the boathouse as well, were painted with enormous red and white stripes, an unexpected and welcome sight after a day chugging from Georgetown in a launch. (It was also a sight which the pilots from Atkinson Field, the American air base, were said to use as a landmark.) The launch that took us there carried supplies from Georgetown as well as groceries, complete with the butler, Sundar. We chugged along canals and creeks, their brown water glittering in the sun, sometimes stopping to look at a coker or dam which needed attention, sometimes looking out over flooded savannahs dense with water-lilies and purple water hyacinths, broken by reefs of palms and tropical forest. Often we went through denser forest where jaguars, wild pigs and wandering alligators lurked. (It was always 'forest' or 'jungle' to us when at Lama, so much more exciting than that commonplace Guianese word 'bush.')

In the school holidays Biddy took a friend with her, sometimes two. As my visits there became more frequent I also took a friend. Those invited to share this Paradise had to be chosen carefully: they had to be the kind whom one sensed would savour the solitude—the savannahs—the winding creeks and the silence. The sunsets— the stars—and again … the silence. There was a lot of silence.… It would be broken by a bird-call or the splash of a fish, maybe a barely discernible slither as an alligator, alarmed by the sight of our boat, slid hastily into the creek. Mostly it was just the soft sound of our paddles dipping in the water. It now seems remarkable how few of our friends met those criteria, how wisely we chose them and how special we became to each other. We were a small select group. We sometimes met, as we grew, in various parts of the world we had never heard of then, we met, we few, to remember and still marvel.

My mother thought that Lama sounded dangerous. To be fair to her, it was. Not only were there snakes—rattlers were the most common—not only was there all that dark brown water, home to alligators and caiman—and the bush, bristling with goodness knew what—but there were all those stories my uncle told at dinner about the people, highly questionable some of them, who had at one time or another worked at Lama. Fortunately, my mother never heard them. Uncle John's favourite dinner starter was the one about Rufus. 'You mean the serial-killer,' we'd correct him, but he'd shake his head sadly. 'No, just a double-killer.' He hated to disappoint us.

Dinner was a splendid affair at Lama. We were miles from anywhere but, in colonial tradition, we were still expected to Dress for Dinner. We girls showered, put on our best afternoon dresses packed specially for the evening (we never dreamed of wearing trousers to dinner) and came down to a table laid with crystal and silver on a white damask cloth. Uncle Johnny was always in a white linen jacket and tie, while Sundar, the butler, was dressed in full butler regalia. The meal was usually freshly caught fish or labba (water haas) and we would ponder the Guianese saying that anyone who ate labba and drank creek water would always return to Guiana. When there were visitors (important visitors to the Colony were frequently taken to see the Water Conservancy), he followed this by saying casually to the dinner party that the delicious labba they'd just enjoyed eating actually belonged to the rodent family.

Over dinner, surrounded by the darkness and the water, my uncle would tell us his tales. He was a gifted teller of tales and the people he spoke of were a gift to any tale-teller.

'Have I told you about Rufus?' he'd ask, and we'd shake our heads because we wanted to hear about Rufus again; every time he told a story it would be more riveting than the time before.

Rufus was convinced that his girlfriend was seeing another man and worked himself into a frenzy about this. The frenzy reached a peak and finally, with shotgun and cartridges stolen from Herman's house (a co-worker) he surprised the girlfriend and her lover at what they were doing (we never heard what) and killed them both. He would have killed the two East Indian men who tried to stop him but his aim was poor and he failed. He failed again when he put the loaded gun under his chin and tried to fire it with his toe. In prison, he pretended that he was unable to speak because of his wounds, but the prison doctor disagreed. Rufus was hanged. Had he succeeded in killing the two East Indians, Uncle Johnny pointed out, he would have been famous throughout the Colony as a serial killer. As it was, he was only a double-killer, two a penny in that far-off, distant, lawless part of the British Empire.

Some of his stories were sad, like the one about Tony, the launch engineer. Tony was half-Chinese and half-something else, and had served in World War I with, of all things, a Highland Regiment. He returned to Guiana shell-shocked and eventually became quite mad. The East Demerara Water Conservancy, in the goodness of their heart, decided to send him to Barbados for six months to recuperate. (In those days, in Guiana, employers did things like that. And Barbados was, of course, a cure that never failed.) But the night before he was to leave Lama, Tony was found hanging in his room....

The darkness around us grew darker as we listened to my uncle's stories, intensely aware of the tropical forest only yards from us and the dark brown water. The fact that a killer had actually worked at Lama—a double-killer!—had rowed the creeks we rowed every day, walked the same paths we walked made us wary of turning around to look into that darkness. It was spooky and we loved it.

'What about Ramatar, the launch engineer after Tony? **Surely** I've told you about **him**?'

His was a particularly sad story. At a cricket match where the umpire declared a batsman LBW and out, the batsman took it badly. Very badly. Prolonged and heated argument followed, as it does at Guianese cricket matches. Ramatar went to make peace, he'd been enjoying the game and was keen for it to go on. The batsman turned on him with an ice-pick and stabbed him in the eye, killing him. Oddly, the killer was found guilty of only manslaughter.

'Time you girls were in bed.' We'd hear this always after the most chilling tale. We went upstairs stamping firmly on the wooden steps and speaking loudly to one another, to convince ourselves that we were not afraid. Not afraid to go to bed with only a hurricane lamp to light us—the generator was turned off promptly at nine—telling each other what we were so often told but never believed, that the creatures around us were even more afraid of us than we were of them. (I was never convinced that I wouldn't wake to see a jaguar peering at me through the mosquito net. I was happy to be small and skinny, convinced I would not make a decent meal.) Usually, we talked bravely or read for a while before turning the lamp off. Being securely tucked up in bed made one very brave indeed. 'Remember … the light attracts them,' my uncle would always say when he told us goodnight.

Neither of us ever asked what.

We were reading one night when when we became aware that a hideous shape was on the mosquito net, picking its way slowly across our line of vision. We lay stiff with fright. The Thing took its time. Both Biddy and I were aware of it even before we set eyes on it, its presence was so powerful. It got closer. Then it was just inches from our noses on the other side of the net … and we had an in-detail view of a horror never before imagined, never before seen—**the underside of a huge tarantula.** The underside was not furry, I think it was in three sections, not twisted or ugly in any way. Just smooth. Very, very smooth. That meant—we realised— that meant it could flatten itself and slide under anything, no matter how low. No matter how low.… It could go anywhere. *Anywhere.*

That was knowledge we could well have done without.

The waters around us were alive with alligators. When the generator went off and we were steeped in darkness we would shine flashlights and pick out their green eyes. They stared back, never blinking. Sometimes, always at night, one of them would get bold and raid the housekeeper's chicken coop; everyone mobilised and chased it with brooms, cutlasses and shrieks. We were not included in the chase.

One night we were awakened by a dreadful splashing.

Flashlights bobbed, hurricane lamps jiggled and people shouted as they rushed out to look. Thoughts of prehistoric water monsters must have been in every mind; such a tumult in the water had never been heard. Then we saw them—a giant camoodi (boa constrictor) and an alligator locked in what was to become an historic battle, an event to be recalled again and again at the dinner table, the story of their death-struggle handed down in the annals of Lama. The snake was wrapped around the alligator, trying impossibly to stretch it and the alligator was snapping back with its terrible jaws, both creatures evenly matched, fighting back without cease, the water alive and foaming in huge circles around them. The struggle went on and on. The alligator could not be stretched and the snake could not be bitten to death. The fight threatened to go on all night, neither creature could possibly have won. Finally someone fetched a gun and shot them both.

Mostly, though, there were moments of quiet beauty. Watching the white cranes fly home in the sunset to their nesting places. Watching the sunset, knowing that each one was special and would never happen again. Perhaps knowing that out there in the world that awaited us, times like these would be times remembered, times to be looked back on and be refreshed by, uplifted and strengthened. Times to be grateful for, for the rest of our lives.

Later, we talked on our bedroom verandah until a late moon rose behind the skeleton tree. We had fallen in love with Rupert Brooke and could quote his poetry by the page. We spoke of that far-off day in England when we would have tea in the Orchard next to the Old Vicarage (we didn't know about the wasps then). We fell asleep to the sound of gently lapping creek water.

We rose to breakfast served by Sundar, we raced to the boat tied up at the landing-stage. We spent mornings, afternoons and dusk on the water.

We talked about our lives, our hopes, our future and that distant time when we would be Old.

We organised everywhere in the world that we knew, excepting, of course, for Lama, which we knew to be perfect.

Chapter Fourteen

We left Enmore and moved to Georgetown when I was twelve. Our parents had been planning this for some time: we would have a small house as a base in town so that Allan and I could go to school daily, and from which my mother could shop at leisure, staying overnight. It had to be small, my mother stressed, because The Kitchen and its occupants were not moving with us. It was also to be our parents' retirement home in due course. Daddy was nearing fifty-five and my mother was determined to get him away from That Place as soon as financially feasible. Until then, Aunt Vic would be in sole charge of the Georgetown house and of Allan, Freddy and me.

Freddy had joined us when I was at boarding-school, the son of my mother's best friend who lived in Venezuela. His father was with an oil company there and Freddy was said to be fluent in Spanish, spoke it like a native, so we were told. I went home one weekend and there he was, being given extra vegetables with particular emphasis on carrots to improve his eyesight, which had to be very good because he was going to be a dentist. His mother was an early believer in vitamins, especially in Vitamin A for the eyes. Freddy was also being educated at Queen's College, like Allan, having lived in Venezuela until then. I expected to pick up Spanish rapidly but sadly, Freddy spoke perfect English and looked at me oddly when I greeted him with 'Olé!'

I was jealous of Freddy, I cannot remember why, and was determined to pretend he didn't exist. I expect it was the sudden emphasis on vitamins, something new to us, and the lengthy discussions between my mother and Aunt Vic about the new additions to our menus. I was not to know I would become a vitamin enthusiast myself. It was formally—and often—declared that if looking after three adolescents turned out to be too much for Aunt Vic—and it would be my fault if it did, everyone knew that—then I would simply have to return to boarding-school. I was out on trial, so to speak.

This plan had been discussed among the adults from time to time, yet when the wheels began to move it was still a surprise to me. It had never occurred to me that there really would come a time when I would not be living at Enmore. A time when the sights, smells and daily sounds, the things that had happened around me since the day I was born, would belong to the past. **My** past. Those things would go on happening but I would not be there to see them. I would no longer be part of them. It was like contemplating death.

I took to walking around the house looking at furniture arrangements, plant-stands with their showering ferns, the horrible stuffed alligator sitting upright on its short back legs—gazing out of windows at different views, regarding the servants wordlessly and at length, to their alarm ('Eh-eh! But what troublin' she!') Telling myself solemnly, 'This—this I shall remember.' Many of the things I was to remember I have forgotten, but I do remember the firm intention to do so.

I had always supposed that we would live in Kingston, Biddy and I took it as read, we both planned and looked forward to that day. All the best people lived in Kingston, it was the most prestigious and without a doubt the loveliest part of Georgetown. All the best parties were held there too and I longed to have party dresses by the dozen as Biddy and her Kingston friends seemed to have. This most upmarket and desirable district was, naturally, by the sea, with wide roads leading up to the Sea Wall, where nannies in panama hats took small children to get the health-giving sea air, Guiana being known throughout the Caribbean as a 'mosquito hole'. There, dogs were walked and there, after sunset, couples did things that were whispered about. Being seen—or even said to be seen!—on the Sea Wall after dark meant ruin to one's reputation. (I know grandmothers, great-grandmothers even, and old men (sometimes not their husbands) of whom it is still whispered *'They were seen together on the Sea Wall after dark....'*)

Large houses stood back from the road, seemingly always freshly painted, surrounded by gardens of the kind I imagined English gardens to look like: green tended lawns, tidily trimmed hedges, splendid shrubs and, to show that this was indeed the tropics, here a fiery blaze of poinciana and there ornamental palms fanning out. And again the grass, unlike the brown spiky grass at Enmore, was green—green—green.

The FitzGeralds lived in Kingston. They had an enormous two-storied wooden house, a lovely house that rambled back and on, with a long, wide verandah in front where, in a huge cage at the far end, Terence's beautiful blue-and-gold toucan loudly demanded homage from all. The brown water of the Lamaha canal rippled by the road. High up in the bedrooms where the sea air drifted in, there drifted too what seemed to me incredibly romantic sounds: the lone bugle from Eve Leary barracks, the Georgetown garrison, and sometimes unbelievably over that distance, the high notes of the Indian Love Call—'When I'm calling YOU—OOo—ooo' sung most beautifully by a gorgeous girl called Stephanie, at the USO Club. Kathleen, Biddy's older sister, flitted from one airy bedroom to another inspecting herself in mirrors, vanishing with a flash of legs in tennis skirts or floating away in shimmering ball-gowns, while Biddy and I gaped at her and admired her and sometimes, when we found our voices, told her how stunning she looked. (She did.) No, there was no question of living anywhere else. Kingston was the only place we could possibly live; Biddy and I discussed it at length and it was all very promising.

'We're going to look at a house that sounds just right,' my mother said when we set off. 'Perfect, in fact.' Perfect, eh? I settled back contentedly in the car. This sounded good. There was no place more perfect than Kingston!

We drove down the coast road, past Kitty Village into Georgetown; we did not turn off and take the well-known route to Kingston but drove on to a part of the town I had never seen before. Ramnarine, the driver, seemed to be lost. He too appeared never to have seen that part before. I simply assumed he was really lost and no alarm bells rang. He kept saying, 'But what dis place?' in a bewildered voice.

What indeed, I wondered as we drove on and on into a Georgetown I had never seen before. 'Where are we?' I asked at last. Bravely. It seemed quite unlike Kingston.

'This is Bourda,' my mother said. 'Not far from the Botanical Gardens and quite close to Queen's College. There is a house for sale here that sounds ideal.'

'BOURDA?!' I had never heard of Bourda. What on earth were my parents thinking of? Surely Daddy … I turned to catch his eye but he would not look at me. Bourda, he told me, still not meeting my eye, had once been a vast plantation in the days of the early colonists, owned by the family of a Dutch military man, General Bourda, who had been prominent in the Colony. The plantation long vanished, the area where it had stood was now geometrically laid out with houses and shops in squares, and busy streets. No wide, tree-shaded avenues here. No remnants of the grand Bourda house. No huge lawns, no poinciana, no royal palms. No, green, green, English-type lawns. Nothing like Kingston. All that remained of Bourda's past grandeur was the cemetery, hideously ornate, where the dead slept in splendour behind solid railings.

I didn't like the look of any of it and shrunk into myself. *This couldn't possibly be happening!* Surely we were always meant to be living in Kingston? So why were we here—looking at a house in this—this—**place?**

This—this *BOURDA!*

Charlotte Street, which we turned into, was unmade-up with no edges. It hardly merited the name of 'street' but was a sort of rough brick road (small pieces of broken rock, that is, not fired red brick) that seemed to alter direction and wander off absently, then suddenly change its mind and rejoin the original layout. It had an odd mixture of houses, some new, some old, some very old indeed and some even seeming to shed bits as we drove by.

I was aghast. I could not speak, I could barely breathe.

We were going to live *here?*

The house where we stopped was two-storied, medium-sized, white-painted. I saw with relief that the front garden was tiny. *Really* tiny. Pocket-handkerchief tiny. It would not do for my mother at all. Not at all, not after her lovely Enmore garden where she always enjoyed spending the cool hours of the day and later relating the magical things being done by her plants. Perhaps it was now time to remind her of the gardens in Kingston? This was just a waste of time, it would never do at all. If I could see it so must she!

'Just the right size of garden,' she said as we walked by to the front steps. Walking by to the front steps didn't take a minute. 'As much as I can manage, without a gardener and a boy. We shall have to do without all sorts of things. All sorts of things!' She had seen the look on my face. 'Your father is going to **retire**, remember. That means he will not have a job, only a pension. Fewer people in The Kitchen—if any!—and a gardener perhaps just once a week—if at all. But what a relief it will be, to get away from That Place!'

I followed in shock.

Every corner of 216 Upper Charlotte Street was occupied by a Chinese family. The lady of the house showed us over it silently, while everyone else went about their business as though we weren't there. A lot of cooking was going on. Daddy muttered something about it needing a good coat of paint inside and out. He didn't seem convinced of its suitability, which cheered me, perhaps Kingston was still possible after all!

Then I saw the tiny room which could—just possibly—make it all worthwhile. It was on the first floor, just off the dining-room and under the stairs. The man who lived in it stood by to let me look around. He didn't say a word, nor did I, but he seemed to know I saw it as a special place and his expression was kind as he watched me. The stairs above gave it an interesting corrugated ceiling, a sloping ceiling made more even interesting by the wide triangular stair landing at the top. An adult could stand upright there. It had a window with a sill protruding a foot or so , with slats on the bottom, and boxed in with carved woodwork. A Dutch window. The one high wall under the landing was shelved from top to bottom and held the man's clothes in tidy piles, together with his other possessions.

This could be my room. There was no rule that said bedrooms had to be upstairs. I could see my books on those shelves, pictures tacked up on the corrugated ceiling, my bed along that wall with a bright counterpane and curtains to match…. Then my mother came in, and I was horrified to hear what she was saying. 'The tinned food and smaller items on the shelves . . .a much better store-room than the one at Enmore. You can actually see everything inside it, no lights needed. It could have been made to order!'

It was going to be a store-room. I knew my cause was lost but I had to say something, if we were really to live here I couldn't let this lovely room become utilitarian and boring without protest.

'It could be my bedroom,' I said hopefully but no one heard me. 'It faces West,' I tried again, 'Very hot, facing West, not good for storing food.' Still, nobody heard. Only the man who lived in the room and his expression changed from kindness to sympathy. Or so I thought.

The viewing over, my mother seemed invigorated, a bad sign I knew instinctively. The woman who had shown us around without a word showed us out just as wordlessly. The busy-ness went on as we left, the peeling, chopping and cooking. Nobody had raised a head as we went in and no one did so as we went out.

This was my first encounter with Chinese aloofness, insularity, separateness, call it what you will. The Chinese were a minority in the colony. They had originally gone there as to work on the plantations but not surprisingly, they quickly extricated themselves from what must have been for them a thoroughly unsatisfactory situation and set up as storekeepers and traders, later providing the Colony with most of its doctors and dentists.

'The Chinese are a race that keep themselves to themselves,' was my mother's explanation when I wondered aloud at their deadpan reception of us—us!—people who were possibly going to buy the house from under their feet! This was news to me. I knew only one Chinese family and they did nothing of the sort, their open friendliness and their hospitality always overwhelmed and silenced me as a small child.

My mother had an old school friend called Del whose family lived in a house at the corner of Norton and Creen Street (another place Ramnarine always had difficulty finding). A house where there was always music—from the radio, the gramophone, the piano, from the three daughters who sang to the music they played, a now-forgotten pastime. Where faces always smiled and everybody laughed and arms stretched out to swoop me up. Where indeed peeling and chopping and cooking did seem to go on all day, where the table was always laden and the house always smelled of incredible food. Upstairs, in the gallery, a card game went on forever among the older men, a silent, intense card game punctuated by occasional shouts of triumph or despair, followed by calls for another bottle of rum. A house where they hadn't heard about keeping themselves to themselves. A lovely house, with lovely people.

Aunt Vic had not been among the party that viewed the house. Back at Enmore, she listened eagerly to Mummy's account of the place and its suitability, nodding her full approval at every detail, keen to have her own base in town, prepared to accept it sight unseen, without a word of criticism. She would go and have a look at it the very next time she was in Georgetown, she said. It sounded much, much more suitable than Kingston and so near to Queen's College too! An excellent position for Allan and Freddy, was her parting taunt at me when she left, all smiles. Kingston, indeed!

And off she went.

Someone spotted her returning from her trip to town, a small figure on that long dirt road. We stood and watched her approach and there was something about her even at that distance, which told us something was amiss. Truly amiss.

The house was all wrong. She didn't like it.

There was *some terrible thing* about it that had upset her, and there was going to be a spectacular volcano-like eruption of words and temper the moment she took her hat off.

And there was.

My aunt wasn't in the door a minute before the volcano erupted. She turned angrily on the person who asked timidly— very timidly—what the Mistress's new house was like.

'What it's like? I'll tell you what it's like! IT'S RIGHT OPPOSITE A N - - - A YARD!'

She flew upstairs to my mother's room where her voice had preceded her. Mummy was ready for her. She held up that restraining hand and wore that I-will-have-none-of-this-kindly-leave-the-room-at-once expression. It worked with everyone but not with Aunt Vic. She stayed put, glaring.

'Please, Vic—the place is a **range-dwelling.** It is due to be demolished very shortly and a block of flats is going up there. Two blocks of flats. The landlord assured us.'

'Due to be demolished, eh!' Hysterical laughter rang through the house. 'Hah! The landlord assured you! Demolished indeed! What a joke! The Colony is full of places that were due to be demolished when Queen Victoria was a girl—and you really think you'll see it happen! Wrong! WRONG! IT WILL NEVER HAPPEN! NEVER, I TELL YOU!'

'When Queen Victoria was a girl' was a much-used expression in Guiana for things that had been promised, improvements we never saw, things that never happened. All, all promised when Queen Victoria was a girl.

This was dreadful.

There was a certain status to being a boarder and living on a sugar plantation, we who did so recognized that when we were very small, without knowing why. I don't suppose those who bestowed that status on us knew either. There was no point protesting to the day pupils that we would much rather live in town and meet our friends after school every day, or walk our dogs on the Sea Wall or go to the pictures when we pleased, free from the restriction of boarding-school rules. No one believed us. We came from another world, a world unknown to most of the girls, many of whom had never set foot on a sugar plantation.

Now, not only was I to lose my standing as a boarder and a plantation-dweller, I was to live RIGHT OPPOSITE A—A—

A range-yard.

I prayed every night that it would be torn down before we moved in. It was bad enough having to tell my friends that I was going to live in Charlotte Street. **Upper** Charlotte Street, I was always careful to stress. It made no difference, not to them and not to me.

It was not Kingston.

'Charlotte Street? Where's that?' they'd ask, blankly.

'In Bourda.'

'**Bourda**?' They hadn't heard of Bourda either. Eventually, I learned that if I said we were going to live near to the Botanical Gardens, that was quite acceptable. Although it **was** rather far from Kingston.

'We shall see blood spilled in that Yard,' Aunt Vic warned before we moved in. 'Those places are awash with blood. Years and years of blood. No one ever lived happily in a—a range-yard. Remember my words! There will be knifings there—killings—and worse.'

What could be worse than killings I did not know, but her words sparked an interest me I never dreamed likely. I had intended to ignore the range-yard, I had meant to pretend it wasn't there, that it didn't exist: that would be my way of dealing with it. Now that I knew it was going to be awash with blood I couldn't take my eyes off it.

The building was long and low like the range-dwellings at Enmore, and ran along one side of the Yard. On the opposite side were the cook-houses, small open lean-to's with a piece of corrugated iron to divide them one from the other, and another piece above for shelter. The Yard itself was a large area of black, trampled earth with a low concrete platform and a standpipe in the middle.

Women flip-flopped loudly from dwellings to cook-houses and several conversations went on at once, everyone free to join in except when out of favour. Then, there would be cries of 'Eh-eh! But who ask she! Look Eye-Pass!'

Water flowed from the standpipe all day. The washing was done here: vegetable-washing, clothes-washing, taken-in washing, people-washing. Two small boys called Austin and Errol were washed several times a day. (Errol was a popular name, Flynn was In, he swashbuckled across the cinema screen and was much admired.) The adults seemed to shower almost as frequently. They brought out a four-sided canvas screen, green and blotchy with mildew, to put around them when they did. Legs were visible and so were heads and shoulders, and conversations carried on uninterrupted.

My mother was as surprised at my interest in the Yard as I

was. 'Don't stand there staring,' she would rebuke me, 'Those people have only one room to live in and most of their lives have to be lived in public, so allow them some privacy. How would you like to be stared at like that?' When she realized I was beyond helping myself she made me close the shutter of the Demerara window.

I watched from upstairs and with the shutter closed I had a perfect view through the slats. It would have been a clear signal to the people in the Yard that they were being watched, if they had cared at all. They didn't. Life in the Yard was more interesting to them than life in the two-storied, white-painted, medium-sized house across the road.

One of the women took in washing. She monopolized the standpipe on Mondays, beating the clothes, splashing suds, and hollering at anyone who showed any sign of wanting to use water. Her washing lines were criss-crossed from one side of the yard to the other and while the clothes dried she warred loudly with the Sweetie Woman and the Channa Lady.

The Sweetie Woman spent whole days and nights in her cook-house making sweets which she peddled in a handcart; they were amazing —Stretchies, a kind of elastic toffee which, with care, could be lengthened to near infinity, Peanut Brittle, packed solidly with whole peanuts—all kinds of crunchy fudge and pink-and-white Coconut Cakes, cone-shaped and succulent. Sweetie Ladies all over the Colony produced these delights and I was overjoyed to find them in Rio de Janiero and Portugal, obviously their home of origin.

The washerwoman claimed that the steam from the sweetie-making clung to the wet washing. How much longer, she demanded, could she go on telling her customers that they only **imagined** their clothes smelled of coconut or butterscotch? People weren't stupid!

The Channa Lady was not to be seen during these arguments though that did not stop tirades being hurled in the direction of her cook-house. Channa has a distinctive smell when peppered or lightly curried, and everyone knew the moment she started cooking even without the despairing screech of the washerwoman to alert the whole neighbourhood.

Boysie was a calming influence, a great diversion, even I looked forward to seeing him from behind my upstairs shutter. He did not live in the Yard but visited regularly and it was not difficult to tell when he arrived. You could hear the smiles in the women's voices, the laughter ready to bubble over.

'Eh-eh! But look who turn up—look trouble!'

'Boysie, you lookin' good f'true! You getting a real Sagarboy!'

Austin and Errol shifted from one foot to the other, admiring him. Boysie wore the whitest of white shirts, white-white trousers and a flashing white smile; he appeared to proposition all the women in the yard. All were stout and middle-aged and they screeched with delight at his suggestions.

'Eh-eh! **What** you say you wan' do to me?'

'Boy, you too young for Big-Woman like me!'

'Boysie, jus' wait till yo' pee mek froth!'

They would carry on laughing long after he left. I could picture him going from one range-yard to another, from one gaggle of admiring little boys to another, spreading laughter and smiles among all those wonderful, undefeated women.

I never saw them go. I did not even know the yard was being vacated. They went one by one, during the day while I was at school. I was vaguely aware that washing was no longer strung across the Yard, and I missed the sound of the Sweetie-Woman's handcart being trundled back at night. That was all.

One afternoon I cycled home from school and found the Yard silent and shut up.

'Where have they gone?' I asked my mother. 'Did they all find somewhere to live?'

The unsatisfactory answer came eventually. 'I expect so. Somewhere would have been found for them.' It was clear that Mummy knew nothing of what had happened to them and where they had gone.

I had never expected to miss them but I was missing them already. The Sweetie Woman and the sound of her handcart trundling back at night. The curry-smell and the screeches that told us all that the Channa Lady had started work. BOYSIE!

How long had they lived there? The range-dwellings were all so ancient; some of those people may well have been born there and their parents too—who knew how many generations had lived and died in those one-room hovels in that black, earth-trodden yard?

'But why did they have to go?"

'The landlord sold the land to a building firm. There will be smart new buildings there soon. It's called Progress, dear. It happens all the time, although in this Colony it happens slowly, I have to admit. The range-dwellings have been there for years, perhaps centuries, it is time they were pulled down and improvements made to the area.'

This was disturbing. Alarming, even. It all sounded so —so callous. 'Can our landlord—? Will we have to move sometime?'

(*Kingston!*)

'No' my mother told me firmly. Very firmly indeed. 'WE have no landlord. This house is ours, your father's and mine. It belongs to us, WE own it, not the Company, the Banks, the Building Societies or the Mortgage Lenders. We will not have to move or to go anywhere else, not unless we want to.'

We both looked out at the deserted range-dwellings where families had lived for years. Perhaps their forefathers had been put there when they arrived on those slave-ships from Africa.

It must have been then that I decided I would have nothing to do with Building Societies, Banks or the Mortgage Lenders. And certainly not with landlords.

The two blocks of flats were large, painted all over in blinding white, and glass louvred. They glittered. When the sun shone on them people who lived on the opposite side of the road closed their shutters. There was a neat side path leading from the front block to the back, a neat very high fence separating them from the rather grand house on the corner, which faced the splendidly-named Oronoque Street. My mother called on the ladies who moved in and they called on her. The visits started with cake and cups of tea and, as the westering sun went down, moved on to glasses of sherry.

One of the ladies, a tired-looking widow, called more often than the others. The widow, Mummy and Aunt Vic spoke in low tones in the drawing room. It was always a 'drawing room' in Guiana, never a 'sitting room' or 'living room' and the word 'lounge' had not yet been heard there. There seemed to be a lot to talk about, always accompanied by long sighs from the widow and exclamations of disbelief and horror from Mummy and Aunt Vic. ('I don't believe!': Mummy. 'I believe anything!': Aunt Vic, considerably more worldly.) The widow began to look even more tired, held her head in her hands a lot and was always offered a 'proper ' drink before she left. ('You've only had two glasses of sherry, dear.')

This called for dedicated eavesdropping which was easy. The schoolroom screen from Enmore now divided the dining room from the drawing room, and my homework was spread out on the dining table. The voices drifted through the screen and the story unfolded day after day, like a serial.

The widow's son was having an affair with the dressmaker who lived in the block of flats at the rear. She was a curvy blonde with a lovely face while the son was a slim, good-looking young man, pale and poetic, with dark eyes. The blonde's husband was unremarkable.

'Who knows how it will all end?' the widow often said dramatically.

One midnight there were shouts and screams from the flats. Shutters opened up and down the street, faces peered out, flashlights waved and jiggled. Cries of 'What's going on?' 'Y'all know what time it is?' 'Is who killin' who?' were repeated up and down the street.

We saw the blonde run barefoot down the side path in a wispy nightdress screaming as she ran, her hair a pale streak in the dark. She carried a lamp in her hand, it wavered and bobbed and lit up the whole unreal scene. Some were sure they had seen blood, all down the front of her nightdress, they swore.

There were cries and screams and a great deal of cursing.

'Come away from the window, Pam!' my mother insisted, 'This is nothing to do with you!'

But I didn't move.

Gradually, the commotion died down. An occasional roar of anger, presumably from the husband, could be heard but at last there was darkness and silence as the lights went out up and down Charlotte Street.

'Well. That's that.' Aunt Vic turned from the window. We'd had a grandstand view. The blonde had run into the tired lady's flat and the door was firmly slammed on the raging husband. 'End of one story. Let's hope the new one is happier.'

I am told that it was indeed happier, that the dressmaker and the poetic young man and the widow, his mother, went to Canada and they all lived there happily and indeed successfully.

When the screams and the shouting had ceased and the houses were dark again, I lay in bed going over it all and I realized that Aunt Vic's prophecy had come true. There had been a knifing opposite us. Blood had flowed … not in the range-yard as she had predicted, but in the new modern flats where the range-yard had stood.

The house in Upper Charlotte Street was never to be the retirement home that my parents planned. Not for my father. The fishing trips to Lama, that idyllic workplace of his brother-in-law Johnny Fitz … the taxidermy he meant to continue studying, the historic sites in the Colony he meant to visit, the books he had been collecting to read … my father did none of it. He hadn't time. Shortly after we moved to Georgetown he became very ill. The news from Enmore reached us one night, a night when a cold wind blew.

Months later, he was dead.

My childhood ended.

Over the years since Independence, Guiana imploded upon itself. The tensions and hatreds that had fermented for centuries erupted, the fall-out went on and on. The country was said to be destroyed, politically, economically, morally, spiritually.

There was mass emigration. People left and went on leaving. Dreadful tales were told, tales of mayhem and murder. There were, as there have always been, as there continue to be, tales of heroism and self-sacrifice, of optimism and hope. There was, in time, resurgence and talk of a brighter future, as there always is, as all people who loved that country knew there would be.

I know now that Guiana has many faces that it shows to people.

To Raleigh and his kind, it was a land that promised enormous wealth, gold enough to clothe yourself in. It was called, after all, El Dorado.

To the explorers it showed jungles with strange beasts and mountains and savannahs with immense rivers and waterfalls. Places to be explored, strange new tribes to be discovered.

Later generations saw opportunities to exploit the land, to grow sugar cane, to grow rich. To add to the glory of the Empire.

There are always missionaries who see it as a place to spread the Word. There is now tourism and people who care about the ecosystem and the animals and who want to show the world the amazing beauty of that strange and wonderful land.

These are just some of the many faces Guiana shows to people.

In the days of my childhood—the days when I was too young to have a past and not old enough to think about the future—in those days of my childhood when I lived only in the immediate present, among people who loved me, among people I loved in the land that I loved—this was the face that Guiana showed to me.

CPSIA information can be obtained
at www.ICGtesting.com
Printed in the USA
BVHW081316180920
589008BV00002B/205

9 781772 441956